COMMUNICATION RISK

COMMUNICATION
RISK

How to Bridge the Client-Advisor Gap
to Protect and Grow Your Business

ELLEN BESSNER

BABIN
BESSNER
SPRY

ISBN 978-1-7753837-0-3 (paperback)
ISBN 978-1-7753837-1-0 (ebook)

Produced by Page Two Books
www.pagetwobooks.com
Cover design by Peter Cocking
Interior design by Taysia Louie
Author photos courtesy of Magdalena Majczak

Every effort has been made to make this book as complete
and accurate as possible, but no warranty or fitness is
implied. The information is provided on an "as is" basis.
The author and the publisher shall have neither liability nor
responsibility to any person or entity with respect to any
loss or damages arising from the information contained in
this book, as it does not constitute legal advice.

19 20 21 22   5 4 3 2

www.babinbessnerspry.com

Previous publications include:

Advisor at Risk: A Roadmap to Protecting Your Business

Dedicated to my mother, Evelyn Bessner.

Acknowledgments

M Y DRIVE, MY determination, and my strength come from my mother, who gave me the encouragement to achieve my career goals.

I would also like to thank my children, Nathan Bessner and Danielle Bessner, and my partner and best friend, Michael Kulbak, for their immeasurable and continuous support and encouragement.

Words cannot describe the support provided by my sister, Merle Bessner (decorator par excellence), who applied her creativity to the choice of title and the cover design and who was there every step of the way to help with every aspect of my book (and my life) that caused me consternation. And on the topic of consternation, Jeff Bessner is my guru and mentor, with never-ending love and support in all facets of my life. And I thank my sister and legal colleague, Ronda Bessner, who has always been my cheerleader, uplifting and motivating me in all aspects of my work and personal life.

And then there are my mentors to thank: Ken Rosenberg, Maureen Jensen, Joel Wiesenfeld, and Rob Granatstein, who make time for me whenever I need their wisdom and support.

It is the confidence my clients have placed in me that has allowed me to develop this fantastic career and to continue it off Bay Street with Cynthia Spry and Ed Babin, two people who bring a completely new meaning to the word 'partner'. Ed and Cynthia have provided me with the continuous support to grow my practice and write this book.

A heartfelt thanks to Kim McPeake, whose constant commitment, strength, and encouragement is irreplaceable.

The content of this book was immeasurably improved by the hard work and dedication of my friend and editor, Pablo Fuchs; by my content editor, Dianne Maley (who was also the content editor of *Advisor at Risk*); and by copy editor Melissa Edwards. Thanks also to Eden Kaill for her edits and final review of the manuscript. Uri Snir for the constant checking of footnotes, references and content, and Shakaira John for the summaries for the "Advisors Take Action" key takeaways in every chapter.

Several readers gave me insightful feedback (read: an insurance policy) on this book and client guide (*Investor's Guide: How to Get the Most from Your Advisor*) before it was finalized: Ruth Mercer (my friend since kindergarten), Cheryl Hamilton (heart of gold), Lorne Switzer (my secret weapon), Shawn Brayman (secret sauce) of PlanPlus, Damienne Lebrun-Reid (brilliant lawyer) of the FPSC, my wonderful new friend and colleague Sarah Bradley of the OBSI, Jan Thompson (Scotia-McLeod advisor), Terry Zavitz (Zavitz Insurance) and Candice Jay (Pembroke Private Wealth).

For not just content, and not just title, and not just feedback on the manuscript, and not just feedback on the first draft of the client guide, and not just responding immediately and being incredibly helpful in every way, I thank Paul Habert.

Finally, thanks goes to cover designer Peter Cocking and Page Two's Trena White and Gabrielle Narsted, who helped me bring this book to market.

—ELLEN

Contents

Introduction *1*

1 The Communication Gap *5*

2 Resolving the Communication Gap *27*

3 Know Yourself *45*

4 Know Your Client *67*

5 Advisor and Client—Know Your Product *93*

6 Client Risk *115*

7 Financial Planning *137*

8 Women Clients *161*

9 Senior Clients *183*

10 Preparing for the Complaint *213*

11 The Investigation *225*

Conclusion *243*

INVESTOR'S GUIDE *246*

Index *261*

Introduction

TEN YEARS AGO, I released my first book, *Advisor at Risk: A Roadmap to Protecting Your Business*, a primer for advisors on understanding risk and setting out a path to safety, with strong emphasis on the paper trail. The book did well (it sold 6,000+ copies) and continues to be relevant today. So why, given that it's a fair amount of work, have I written another one?

There is a critical aspect to the advisor-client relationship that was outside the scope of *Advisor at Risk*, and that's the importance of clear, meaningful communication. In my many years as a litigation lawyer, I have seen so many distressed advisors spend countless hours fighting in court over client losses. Sometimes the complaints were due to the advisor misunderstanding the client's risk profile, and sometimes it was because the client was misleading. But whatever the surface cause, the root cause is the same: the failure of both parties to properly understand and communicate.

The communication gap is what gets most advisors into trouble—and the trouble can be deep. This book unpacks this widespread problem and offers solutions for better communication with clients. It's a deeper examination of the gap between clients and advisors, and it will help in a completely different way than my first book did.

Along with this book, I have also produced an accompanying guide, titled *Investor's Guide: How to Get the Most from Your Registered Advisor*, that is intended for you to offer to clients as a way to show that they have everything to gain by understanding the importance of clear communication and transparency with their advisors or agents. A sample of this client guide appears in the back of this book, and is also available for download on our website for you to distribute to your clients, to help them gain the tools they need to hold up their end in closing this dangerous gap. I must emphasize, however, that it is you—whether you are an investment advisor, mutual fund advisor, insurance agent, planner, dealing representative, or portfolio manager—who steers the relationship. That's what this book is intended to help you do.

Many think of the advisor and the client as being on opposite sides of the table, with the advisor seeking to get the most money possible from the client without regard for the client's interests. I don't see it this way, and I don't think this is true of most advisors. Both advisor and client are on the same side and want the same thing: for the client to succeed in their financial goals. This is why I wrote this book for advisors and the guide for clients—to help advisors and clients understand each other better, and to create a future with fewer unhappy clients, fewer complaints, and even fewer lawsuits.

Throughout this book, and using real (and very disguised) case studies, I look at different high-risk situations and types of clients an advisor or agent can encounter, and what specific communication gaps can arise in each case. By unpacking and exploring these situations, and by laying out strategies for better understanding your client—and your client better understanding their role—I will help you close the gap and set the foundation for far more fulfilling advisor-client relationships.

It's also important to note that *Communication Risk* is not just for advisors. Readers of this book may include supervisors, assistants, and executives, whether in a compliance role or not, in the financial services industry. Note that regardless of how the regulators refer to these different types of advisors, this book will generically refer to them all as 'advisor'.

For those of you who have read *Advisor at Risk*, you will recognize the action lists that I employ at the end of each chapter. If you have not yet read my previous book (and I recommend you do!), don't worry. This book stands on its own.

My ultimate goals with *Communication Risk* are that advisors and clients gain a fresh outlook, new strategies, and a renewed commitment to clearer and fuller communication and that they, their supervisors, and the companies they work for are equipped with the tools they need to reduce their risk. I hope that everyone in the financial services industry who reads this book—and their clients who read the accompanying client guide—share a new perspective that will help bridge the gap and avoid unnecessary and expensive litigation and regulatory actions. This will make for a more beneficial industry for all of us.

Finally, a note to my non-Canadian readers: while this book uses many Canadian examples and mentions certain Canadian financial products, regulations, and institutions, please know that these are simply illustrations. The concepts

I explore are universal and will certainly apply to you and your client relationships.

THIS BOOK IS not a legal text. For ease of reading, the legal principles most often relevant to this industry have been described in broad, general strokes. In regard to specific issues of concern, you will need to seek legal advice. I do, however, present and analyze many examples, mostly from what I have observed in my practice, in the hope that you will learn from the mistakes of others. The examples illustrate common reasons for a communication gap between advisors and clients. I have changed the examples from my practice so that even if these clients read this book, they would not be able to identify their own circumstances.

1

The Communication Gap

I. What Are the Causes of the Communication Gap?

I have spent more than 25 years defending advisors in litigation and regulatory matters, and in that time I have found that the main source of problems is the gap in understanding and communication between advisors and their clients. Where clients are secretive, advisors fail to draw them out; where clients expect too much, advisors fail to manage those unreasonable expectations. In this chapter, I will explore how the communication gap arises and what the consequences can be.

First, we'll look at three case studies: Dank, an investor who lost big money chasing big returns without giving enough thought to the risks; Flank, an investor who didn't save enough for retirement and hoped to make up the difference with higher-risk investments; and, finally, Shank, a client who was assumed to be so well off that the advisor was not comfortable asking the questions necessary to ensure she qualified for the investment. All three cases—and many others throughout this book—are real-world examples from my own experience as a litigator that portray common communication gaps between clients and advisors. For all, I have altered the details to the point where each case will be unrecognizable even by the people originally involved.

Example 1: Dank

Dank is arguably one of the most treacherous kinds of clients an advisor can have, because he pretends to be wealthier than he actually is. Dank is a highly educated professional in his early 50s, married with four children. He works hard and plays hard. Dank earns well but has expensive habits and expensive toys, such as cars and boats. He hopes to inherit money from his parents one day, but that is uncertain. While he has all the trappings of wealth, Dank is actually in dire straits. He might not have enough money to pay for his children's private school fees this year. He is deep into his line of credit and his credit cards. He hopes winning big in the stock market will help him out of his bind.

Dank calls up his advisor and asks for some high-return strategies he has read about. "Do you realize these investments are risky?" his advisor asks. "Sure," Dank replies in his quest for big gains, playing down any concern for potential risks. He's desperate. The advisor presses a bit but gives up when Dank stops responding and grows evasive.

Dank's advisor could ask: "How much can you afford to lose?" But he doesn't. Instead, he ignores the red flags and recommends a high-risk, diversified portfolio of securities. Months pass and things go from bad to worse. Dank bails at a huge loss.

Dank is angry and decides to switch advisors. The new advisor, eager to get Dank's account, fails to look into what happened between Dank and his previous advisor. She promises Dank better results, and the new advisor doesn't stop there. She suggests Dank call me, knowing that I practice law in this area, to explore suing his previous advisor.

"I wanted to make money, not lose it," Dank says to me during our first and only telephone conversation. "That's why I hired an advisor in the first place."

Dank acknowledges that he told his previous advisor he was prepared to take the necessary risks to earn better returns. I tell Dank that, having chosen to invest in high-risk stocks, he took his chances and lost. Dank replies that he didn't realize he was taking such a big risk and that he could lose so much money. I tell him that I won't take his case. I mostly represent advisors, and, anyway, Dank doesn't have much of a case because he made a choice. He was knowledgeable and sophisticated enough to understand that he was taking big risks, hoping this would make him money.

Dank finds another lawyer and sues his former advisor and the dealer for $1 million. If only Dank's advisor had explored Dank's risk profile in earnest and managed his unrealistic expectations.

Example 2: Flank

Flank is in his 60s. He is divorced with three grown children. Flank has not saved enough for his retirement, but he is in denial. He continues to travel and enjoy life. He has some savings in an RRSP but not nearly what he would need to retire in the lifestyle to which he is accustomed. He decides that he should see a financial planner to help him plan for a comfortable retirement, and meets with an advisor recommended to him by his neighbor. The advisor says she can help build a plan for Flank, as well as invest his money in mutual funds and segregated funds. The advisor collects information from Flank and quickly gathers that Flank has not saved enough for his retirement. She tells Flank that his only option is to substantially reduce his spending so he can save more and invest prudently in conservative funds. Flank is not satisfied with this alternative, especially after he and the advisor discuss the types of returns that conservative funds will yield. Such low yields will clearly not do the trick, says Flank, and he asks what investments will yield better returns. The advisor explains the other types of funds available, and shows Flank the returns these other funds have yielded in the past one, three, and five years. Flank is excited about the prospect of more attractive returns and tells the advisor that this is what he wants to invest in. The advisor explains that with higher returns come higher risks, but Flank says he has no option.

The advisor does not delve into what could happen to Flank if the market doesn't co-operate. She doesn't explain that past returns are no guarantee of future returns, even though this is printed on the fund fact sheet and in the prospectus. The advisor doesn't take detailed notes or send an email to Flank warning him of the potential risks and reaffirming that her advice is for Flank to tighten his belt and start saving and investing conservatively. Instead, accounts are opened, showing medium-high risk and a "good" level of sophistication. Investments are made in medium- to high-risk mutual funds and segregated funds. Very little is discussed about the cost of the funds, but information is emailed (the fund facts) and mailed (the prospectus and other materials). Flank closely watches his statements and sees a dip in the value of two of the four funds. Flank gets anxious. Matters don't improve. Flank grows more impatient and launches a complaint with the Ombudsman for Banking Services and Investments (OBSI). The OBSI investigates and, because Flank's advisor failed to caution him and keep a record of having explained the risks to Flank, it finds in favor of Flank.

So what went wrong? Did the advisor caution Flank enough? Should she have communicated this in writing to Flank? Would the advisor have been wise to not accept Flank as a client if Flank refused to follow a more balanced plan?

Example 3: Shank

Shank is believed to be a high-net-worth client and belongs to a very exclusive golf club. Another member of the club, a portfolio manager, happens to golf with Shank and recommends that she invest in one of his high-risk pooled funds,[1] bragging about the amazing returns. Shank is introduced to one of the advisors at the dealer distributing the pooled fund whose responsibility is to meet with clients to open accounts. Shank expresses to the advisor that she is unwilling to invest with the firm if she must share information about her assets. Further, the portfolio manager who referred Shank also tells the advisor that no questions are to be asked. This has happened before on many occasions, so the advisor knows the drill. He obediently shows Shank the form to sign and has already checked off that Shank has more than $1,000,000 in

---

1   If you are selling pooled funds, see: OSC Staff Notice 33-748:2017, "Annual summary report for advisors, dealers, and investment fund managers"; ASC Notice 33-705, "Exempt market dealer sweep report"; and CSA Staff Notice 31-336.

investable assets (and so meets the financial asset test, one of the tests required to qualify the client as an accredited investor and entitle her to invest in the pooled fund[2]). The advisor does not ask Shank any questions to confirm that she actually meets this benchmark.

Later, when the advisor is audited by the regulator, there are no notes or records to support that Shank is actually an accredited investor—and other client files show the same lack of detailed records. The securities regulator imposes terms and conditions that require the advisor and his entire firm to step up their game in communicating with clients and in taking notes that support their selections on the qualifying forms.

The firm does not adhere to the conditions the regulator sets. At the next regulatory audit, the matter is referred to enforcement.

THE EXAMPLES OF Dank, Flank, and Shank represent the three main causes for the communication gap between the client and the advisor: advisors fail to manage their clients' expectations; advisors take their clients' assertions at face value; and clients are evasive or even secretive about their personal financial situation.

Let's look at all three of these causes in turn.

A. Clients may have unreasonable expectations

People go to professionals when they have a problem that they don't know how to resolve by themselves. They pay a person

---

2   CSA's NI 44-106 Prospectus Exemptions accredited investor exemption financial asset test requires the advisor to have evidence that the client has $1,000,000 in financial assets less liabilities.

who has education and experience that they do not have. They go to doctors in the hope that a doctor can cure what ails them; they go to lawyers to win their legal battles or to get help completing a transaction; they go to accountants in the hope of paying lower taxes. However, whether the doctor finds a cure or not, whether the lawyer wins the case or not, whether the accountant saves them money or not, these professionals get paid. In most professional-client relationships, there are no guarantees of success, and success is not a condition of payment.[3]

Like most other professionals, whether advisors make or lose the client money, they get paid for the advice rendered. However, unlike with payments to other professionals, who may not necessarily have resolved their problems, clients seem particularly annoyed about paying advisors when they lose money in their accounts.[4]

But paying an advisor is not the same thing as tipping a waiter for good service, or not leaving a tip when the service is bad. Payment to professionals is not conditional upon results.

The job of a professional is to listen to the client, ask the right questions, analyze the problem, and apply their expertise to help resolve it or help the client achieve their goals. I use the word "help" because the professional is not a magician. They do not always have the solution. Accordingly, professionals need to manage their clients' expectations so that they are

---

3   In certain circumstances a lawyer works on a contingency basis so no legal fees are paid unless the client wins the case, but these terms are clear to the client and are set out in a letter of retainer, which serves as a contract.

4   Client relationship model (CRM) disclosure rules mean we are entering an era where clients will understand that regardless of results, advisors get paid.

reasonable. Professionals need to clearly explain to their clients that what might be achieved cannot be guaranteed. They need to explain what can be resolved and what cannot, what might be the outcome and what might not.

A doctor, for example, will prescribe cream for a rash but might not be certain this will resolve the problem. So, they might say to the patient: "Here is some cream for that rash. If it doesn't go away in three days, come back to see me so we can explore this more deeply." This doctor is managing the patient's expectations. While the doctor is prescribing this particular cream because the rash presents as one that might be resolved with such a prescription, it may not work. The doctor explains this, and suggests a second step in case it does not. Advisors need to take a similar approach, all the while managing the client's expectations.

Over the past several years, the role of the advisor has evolved from recommending products (e.g., stocks, bonds, mutual funds, life insurance, segregated funds, hedge funds, pooled funds) to encompassing a more holistic approach, examining the client's entire financial situation. Even with this important shift, a substantial number of clients continue to measure their advisor's performance by one criterion and one only: how much money they have made or lost. These are the clients who are most likely to complain when markets turn against them and they lose money because they did not allow time for the market to recover.

Such evaluations are not realistic or reasonable, since short-term returns are dependent on short-term market performance. Instead, clients should look at the entire picture, including the value of all services provided by their advisor over a longer period. Because there cannot be a guarantee of success,[5] a client's expectations need to be carefully managed throughout the entire relationship to avoid surprises or disappointment. The number-one reason, in my experience, why clients sue their advisors is that they are surprised when their portfolios turn out to be riskier than they wanted—even if the investments were consistent with the risk profile set out in their Know Your Client (KYC) forms.

I can't tell you how many times my own advisor has told me during an annual portfolio review, when she is reporting good results, that there are no guarantees for the following year. She reminds me of my risk profile and my personal goals. She makes the point that we are not striving to knock the ball out of the park but simply to get solid, reasonable, consistent returns over the long term.

So how can advisors avoid facing unhappy clients like Dank, Flank, or Shank? From the beginning of the relationship, advisors need to consistently and continually ensure that they know their clients and that they are managing their clients' expectations. Clients, in turn, need to keep their expectations in check. The responsibility is on both parties.

B. What the client says isn't necessarily what the client means

Sometimes, clients express their personal goals, expectations, and risk profile emphatically, and so advisors accept them at face value. The problem is that what the client says may not

---

5   There are exceptions for certain products that might guarantee that you will not lose your principal, or for guaranteed investment certificates that are guaranteed by an institution that should be able to pay it back on maturity (not all GICs are backed by solid organizations).

be accurate or may not be the entire picture. Clients may be pretending to be wealthier or more knowledgeable than they actually are. Or they may not fully grasp the risk involved in a particular investment because they have not had their risk profile tested in a severe market downturn. Either way, it can make for a rocky foundation in both the choice of investments and the ongoing advisor-client relationship.

What often happens in these circumstances is that, if the account results are disappointing, the client turns against the advisor and blames them, demanding that losses be repaid, threatening litigation, and complaining to the regulator.

Even clients who seem to know their goals and articulate them clearly may not realize how their risk profile can change with circumstances or the market. They may also be embarrassed to admit that they are nervous and less knowledgeable than they appear. For example, what are the client's expectations and understanding when they say they have a "high risk tolerance"?[6] Are they prepared to lose money? How much? Can the client afford to lose money? Dank told his advisor his risk profile was high, but was he prepared for losses if the investments didn't pan out? It certainly didn't seem that way.

Dank thought that if he put all of his money into high-risk investments and the results were favorable, then that would solve his financial problems. The trouble is, Dank (and Flank, too) couldn't afford to lose any money. So it was up to the advisor to probe into what Dank meant by high risk. The advisor should have explored with Dank why he wanted to put all his money into high-risk investments. Surely, this was a red flag. The advisor should also have determined whether Dank could afford to take the risk of the potential losses.

---

6   A further and deeper review of risk profiles will be explored in Chapter 6.

This is a typical situation in which clients need to be saved from themselves. The advisor in this case might have believed that Dank was experienced and knowledgeable and that he understood himself and the market. But the advisor was wrong not to explore with Dank what his motivations were for taking so much risk. The advisor should have gained a fuller understanding of Dank's financial picture, and ensured that when Dank said he wanted high-risk investments, he meant that he could afford the losses. If he had probed, he presumably would have learned that Dank needed to make money in the market to pay for luxuries he was consuming but could not really afford. It is possible that Dank might have deflected any attempt by the advisor to probe into his affairs, because he didn't want to reveal that desperation was behind his desire to take big bets. However, the advisor should have been prepared for such deflection, particularly at the beginning of the relationship when the client didn't yet know him well enough to be open and transparent about his worries or bad habits.

C. Clients may be secretive

A serious problem in this industry is that there can be a lack of trust and co-operation between clients and their advisors. Advisors might fail or neglect to probe further, regardless of the client's attitude.

On one side, clients can be secretive, misleading the advisor or omitting personal information. Advisors need to appreciate the risks of working with such a client. With a secretive client, advisors are forced to make recommendations based upon broad statements that may not be accurate. If the information is wrong because the client was being vague about their income or net assets, the client may later be able to prove that the information contained in their KYC form and financial plan was untrue. This, of course, gives the client an upper hand when suing the advisor or complaining to the regulator.[7] If a client or prospective client is secretive, beware of these risks if you intend to continue to work with them!

On the other side of the equation, the advisor is obliged to probe further when a client is vague or seems to be telling stories. An advisor who merely accepts a client's statements as fact, without asking for additional information, accepts that the client-advisor relationship will continue to be based on mistrust and misapprehension: mistrust by the client, who is unwilling to be transparent, and misapprehension on the part of the advisor, who should know this client is trouble.

Dank misled his advisor when he told him that he had a big appetite for risk. After he lost a substantial sum, Dank became a very dissatisfied client and sought a new advisor. (For this reason, advisors need to be wary of clients who jump from one advisor to another, particularly after suffering recent losses.) Mistrust and misapprehension are not good foundations for a relationship of any kind, including one between a client and an advisor.

II. Communication Breakdown

A communication breakdown can end in grief for both the advisor and the client. Here's what often happens, using Dank's case as an example.

---

7   While the client will not necessarily win on these facts, the cost and stress of litigation and regulatory matters are better avoided altogether.

A. The client lodges a complaint

Dank is angry and wants to get his money back, so he hires a lawyer. The lawyer writes to the advisor and his dealer setting out the basis for Dank's complaint.

Like many clients who sue their advisor for investment losses, Dank asserts that his investments were too risky given his risk profile.[8] He is suing for $1,000,000. Dank insists that, given how he was cash-strapped and had financial obligations in the short term, he could not afford to lose any of his capital. The details he provides to his lawyer include his assets and liabilities at the time the account was opened, as well as the changes in his financial position over the years he was invested with the advisor. For all of these circumstances, Dank asserts that the investments were unsuitable, the most common foundation for a claim in advisor-client litigation.

Dank asserts that the information on the KYC form was defective at the time the account was opened, and was not updated to reflect changes in his financial situation during the period he invested with the advisor. When he first opened the account, Dank had told his advisor that his income was $350,000. But his income later dropped to zero when Dank lost his job, unexpectedly, one year later. Throughout this period, his advisor neglected to inquire if there had been any changes, didn't update the KYC form, and never adjusted the investments to reflect this significant change. Dank couldn't find a job commensurate with his previous income and responsibilities, so a year later he became a consultant, earning $65,000 a year, with the hope that this income would ultimately increase over time.

---

8   See Chapter 6 for more on 'risk profile' and why I don't refer to it as 'risk tolerance'— the term the financial industry usually uses.

The KYC form, which bears Dank's signature, allowed for 100% high-risk investments. It indicated that Dank's income was between $350,000 and $450,000 and his assets exceeded $2,000,000. Dank denies that this information was accurate, both at the time the account was opened and afterward. Further, Dank states that, while his assets may have exceeded $2,000,000, he was so highly leveraged (because of his expensive lifestyle) that his net worth was in the red.

Dank signed one KYC form when he opened the account, and was never asked to fill out an updated form throughout the two years that he was invested with his advisor, even after he lost his job. Moreover, there were no notes in the file about any meetings that the advisor had with Dank. There was nothing confirming what was said and nothing indicating that the advisor had probed into Dank's statements. There was no evidence that Dank could afford to take risks.

B. The dealer investigates Dank's complaint

Upon receiving Dank's complaint, the dealer is required to carefully review it and investigate all paperwork. The dealer asks the advisor relevant questions associated with the allegations. In this case, the dealer asks for Dank's notes, emails, and letters. They also review the account documents and statements to determine whether the complaint has any merit.

After the dealer carefully examines the paperwork and the allegations in the complaint, they send emails to the advisor and a few other involved parties, asking specific questions that need responses in writing. In various cases, dealers send emails, hold interviews, or both, depending on what is needed. This exchange will likely be subject to review by the regulator, so the dealer's investigators need to be very careful about how this is done.

While an advisor may be the main witness, the paper trail they prepare throughout the relationship with the client is usually the key to whether they and the dealer win or, as in this case, the advisor and dealer have to pay Dank's claim.

C. The advisor responds to Dank's complaint

There are many things that Dank's former advisor will likely tell the compliance department or lawyer (me), and many possible responses from the client and their lawyer in cases where the paper trail is thin or nonexistent. Here's a list of likely responses from the client's lawyers or how a judge or regulator might conclude.

i. The advisor says: "The client signed the KYC form; I relied on his signature and so should the judge."

Response: A signed Know Your Client form alone is not enough; more than just a client signature is needed.

In my representation of advisors, I am regularly asked why I suggest that the client signatures on the KYC forms are not enough to prove the veracity of the information on the forms. This question is usually in the context of a client complaint that needs to be defended either in front of the regulator or in litigation. The question indicates the advisor doesn't have a clear understanding of the purpose of the KYC form.

As all advisors know, there is a regulatory and legal obligation to know each client at every stage of the client-advisor relationship. That is the reason for the KYC form. However, the duty to know your client goes far beyond the questions on the KYC form. This form is merely a summary of what the advisor learned about the client. Without a paper trail describing what else the advisor learned that supports the entries on the form, even if the client has signed it, the advisor is left with no proof that what was on the form is supportable with evidence.

In this example, Dank denies the income and asset information that is listed on the form. He asserts that the listed income is wrong not only because he lost his job but also because he never made between $350,000 and $450,000. Dank asserts that the advisor never asked him this question, and suggests that maybe the advisor just made an assumption rather than having a meaningful discussion about Dank's present and anticipated income.

The advisor is left to prove that what is on the KYC form accurately reflected Dank's income, information that was collected during their first meetings. However, he has no notes to prove that they even had a discussion about Dank's income. It may be that the advisor asked and Dank didn't want to tell him, so they agreed to check off the highest bracket of income on the form. Or it could be that the advisor did ask, but Dank was evasive. There are no notes in the advisor's file to support either theory. All we know is that the number is wrong. Dank supplied his tax returns in the litigation to prove that his income was $150,000 a year before he was fired.

So, with a client signature and nothing else, without proof that the client provided this information to the advisor, the advisor is unable to prove that he relied on the client's information to prepare the KYC form, or that he asked Dank any questions. Without this paper trail, the information on the form will not be believed by either a judge or a regulator. This is why advisors need to spend the time required to get to know their clients thoroughly, and prepare a paper trail of what they learned through this process. (We will explore this in more detail in Chapters 2 and 5.)

Even if the advisor had verbally asked Dank the same question that appears on the KYC—"What is your annual income?"—that still would have been insufficient detail to prove that he knew his client. A simple answer that permits the advisor to complete the form by filling in numbers ignores numerous facts that might be relevant to getting to know the client.

For example, the advisor could have asked Dank how many years he had made this sum of money in the past, and what he expected to be earning in future.[9] Dank could have considered and shared with his advisor how secure his job was and whether there was any current threat of termination. Without having sought out this information, the advisor now cannot prove that he explored the real facts behind his client's financial situation.

Because Dank's advisor had not asked the appropriate questions, it was next to impossible to now prove that the investments were suitable. Accordingly, settling the complaint by paying the client might be the advisor's best option.

ii. The advisor says: "The client understood all the trades; in fact, these were the client's ideas!"

Response: There are two questions to ask arising from the advisor's assertion. First, does the advisor think that proving

---

9   Note that when selling investment funds without a prospectus to accredited investors pursuant to securities laws, these are the types of questions you need to ask when using the income exemption. There is no reason you shouldn't ask them in other situations, too, in order to ensure you know the client.

a client understood the trades is sufficient defense against a complaint alleging that the investments were unsuitable? And, second, is there a paper trail showing what the client and advisor discussed, and proving that the client initiated the investment and had the capacity to understand the risks?

For the first question, regardless of their sophistication, clients usually assert that they relied on their advisors to choose suitable investments. The reason advisors are retained by clients, and paid by them, is to choose investments in keeping with the client's risk profile. So, if the investments were unsuitable, the regulatory and legal framework will support the client's case that losses associated with unsuitable investments were the advisor's fault.

The onus is on the advisor to prove either that the investments were consistent with the client risk profile, or that the trade was 'unsolicited' and therefore the client's idea (and that the client understood the implications of this). For example, the advisor may have a paper trail indicating that the trade was the client's idea, which makes the trade unsolicited. The advisor may also have evidence that the client had the ability and sophistication to understand the risks, or that he did in fact understand them in this situation. If the advisor has both of these—and I have been involved in cases where such evidence existed—then the advisor may have a strong argument that the risk was known and undertaken by the client. However, without this evidence, it will be difficult to prove that the losses associated with any unsuitable investment are not the responsibility of the advisor.

Of course, if the advisor has proof that the client had substantial experience and/or a background in trading, and was initiating trades on a regular basis, then that would help to shift at least a portion of the blame, if not all of it, onto the client.[10]

iii. The advisor says: "The client told me this was his play money."

Response: Well, if Dank really said this, there are the following three questions to ask. What is the advisor's proof that Dank said this? What did the advisor do to test whether it was true? And does the advisor have a paper trail with this proof?

We might know that Dank was materialistic and a show-off with a fancy car and other assets leveraged to the hilt. But did the advisor collect the necessary information to prove that Dank could indeed afford to lose the money he invested in the high-risk securities? In this case, the advisor did not ask about Dank's debt—his mortgages, lines of credits, loans, or credit cards—so there is no evidence to ascertain whether or not Dank was able to afford to use the funds he invested as play money.

If Dank was not forthcoming when the advisor attempted to probe the veracity of his assertion that this was money he could afford to lose, then the advisor should have at least sent an email to Dank noting that Dank had told the advisor he could afford to lose the money invested.

---

10 Each province in Canada has its own legislation that permits the apportionment of damages among the plaintiff and defendants in an action based on negligence. However, note that the apportionment of damages is not an option for portfolio managers or others who exercise discretion in a client account. Since this book is not a legal text, I will not explore this in detail.

iv. The advisor says: "The client told me that he was prepared to take risks to get higher returns."

Response: Regardless of what a client says they want, advisors need to test the statement and refuse the demand for high risk if it is their assessment that high-risk investments are unsuitable. Whether a client can afford to lose money is an important determination. Could Dank, who was cash-strapped and on the eve of some substantial school fee payments, afford to lose money? If a patient tells a doctor what medication they want, the doctor still has the duty to examine the patient to ensure that the medication is appropriate, regardless of any pressure from said patient. Whenever an advisor is faced with a client who says what they want in their account and does not permit the advisor to properly explore with them the suitability of the investment, the advisor would do well to consider this analogy of the doctor. Doctors and advisors both have the professional obligation[11] to get to know each client (akin to a doctor's examination, in which the doctor asks many questions), ascertain what the client needs (akin to a medical diagnosis), and then recommend what is suitable (akin to a doctor's prescription). The advisor has the same obligation.

v. The advisor says: "The client was only 40 years old when he started trading with me and had a substantial income."

Response: That may have been the case when the advisor first met Dank, but it was not the case when Dank lost his job. Why didn't the advisor know that Dank had lost his job? Because Dank was too proud to share this information with him. If the advisor had a paper trail showing he'd asked Dank whether

---

11   *Rhoads v. Prudential-Bache Securities Canada Ltd.* (1992), 63 BCLR (2d) 256 (BCCA) at 262.

anything had changed and that Dank had not shared this change with him, I suggest that the advisor would have had an argument that the account could not be adjusted to reflect changes that the client chose not to disclose. However, being 40 and having a substantial income is only a small piece of the puzzle. The rest of the client's personal financial situation is important—things such as cash flow, debt, and present and anticipated financial obligations.

In this situation, I would meet with the advisor and review all of the reasons why he didn't want to pay Dank a dime to settle the matter, challenging Dank's evidence or lack thereof. The advisor may come around to observe the weaknesses in his case. Alternatively, I may be able to collect sufficient data to appreciate why the advisor might be right—particularly if he has the necessary paper trail.

YOU CAN SEE how the consequences of the communication gap can be serious and cause the advisor and dealer significant stress, along with both monetary and reputational damage. Below are some immediate action steps you can take; in the next chapter, we will look in greater depth at what advisors can do to avoid or overcome the communication gap.

Summary

The communication gap is the main cause of client complaints against their advisors. To avoid or minimize the communication gap and its consequences, it is crucial for advisors to know their clients and to maintain a paper trail throughout the relationship.

Advisors Take Action

✓ Consistently and continually ensure you know your clients.

✓ Continuously manage your clients' expectations through-out the relationship by clearly explaining to your clients that what might be achieved cannot be guaranteed.

✓ Don't simply accept what clients are prepared to tell you on a superficial level; dig into their personal goals and expectations to ensure you get the full picture.

✓ Spend the time required to get to know your clients thoroughly, beyond the questions on the KYC form, and prepare a paper trail of what you learned about your clients through this process.

✓ Remember, for any investigation into a client complaint, the paper trail you prepared throughout your relationship with the client is key to the strength of your defense.

2

Resolving the Communication Gap

I N THE LAST chapter, we looked at some serious real-world examples of communication breakdown that led to client complaints and the potential for the advisor and dealer to pay a big price both financially and reputationally. Now that I have your attention, let's look at a number of strategies for drawing out clients and avoiding these problems.

First, though, it's worth reviewing the kind of challenges you might face with secretive or disengaged clients.

Mr. Mookey is referred to you by one of your high-net-worth clients. You are told that he has at least two investment advisors, as well as commercial and residential real estate holdings. Mr. Mookey meets with you. He certainly doesn't appear to be a man of means. His clothes are plain, his watch is inexpensive, and you cannot help but notice that his shoes need polishing. He tells you that he would like to add one more advisor to make it three. You begin to ask him about his other advisors and what he is looking for in a third. He tells you that you don't have to worry about asking him questions; he will do the asking. He proceeds to ask you about your expertise and how you are compensated. Then he abruptly ends the meeting, telling you he needs to leave because he has other obligations. You assume he didn't like your answers, but you politely see him out and offer him your business card, which he declines to take. "Wow, I really must have bombed," you think to yourself.

For the next several weeks, you replay the meeting in your head and worry that Mr. Mookey will tell the referring client something negative about you. Then, out of the blue, Mr. Mookey calls and tells you to send the client account documents. The only thing Mr. Mookey is interested in discussing is the fee, but just as you begin to explain, he abruptly interrupts you and says that he has to go and that he will be waiting for the documents. He'll be looking for suggestions about how to invest the $750,000 discussed, with another $500,000 to come in about a week.

Needless to say, you are elated. After doing a happy dance around the office, you settle down to prepare the documents. You have absolutely no information about the client, and you are worried that the client may end up signing forms that have only been partly completed. You'd have to send them back to him for completion and initialing, introducing another problem. So you fill in what you can, and guess at the rest. The documents are sent and returned, signed by the client, who sends you the money to invest. Over time, Mr. Mookey warms up to you but never seems to have the time to discuss the account, his plan, or his own expectations.

The day the money arrives to deposit into Mr. Mookey's account is a happy day for you. But it will end up being a sad day in your memory after, inevitably, the truth is revealed: you didn't know your client, and didn't insist that he share the information required to enable you to open the account properly and invest suitably.

While this is an extreme example, there are many others that I have seen in which the client never makes the time for the advisor, and never shares information that the advisor needs to ensure the account is managed in a manner consistent with the client's needs and that fits in well with the client's other assets. Clients can be secretive and unengaged, so advisors need the skills to be able to figure out how to deal with them and get the necessary information. With the pressures advisors face today to increase their business, few advisors will turn away high-net-worth clients, even if they are being secretive.

Here is a less extreme example: Dr. Fruit is exhausted from working long hours and taking care of her two children and her elderly parents. She is from a culture that is secretive about assets, and she is not forthcoming even with her own advisor. While she only has a limited amount of time to spend, she makes a few minutes for you from time to time. But the bigger problem is that she remains unengaged in the process and is unwilling to share personal information with you.

In both of these examples, Mr. Mookey and Dr. Fruit, you will have to look for ways to get the information you need to mitigate your risk. What follows are a few strategies you can employ for each type of situation.

I. The Advisor and Client Do Not Spend Enough Time to Help the Advisor Know the Client

It can take time to get to know a person well, particularly well enough for the client to feel comfortable sharing personal information. Clients also need to feel comfortable enough to ask questions that might make them appear uninformed, which could embarrass them. This can be hard to do if either the advisor or client is rushing through the initial meeting or those that follow.

Clients may be rushing because they are juggling personal, work, and other obligations, but the client is not the only person who may rush through a meeting. Sometimes advisors have not scheduled enough time to properly discover the client's full financial picture. Further, some portfolios are so small that the advisor doesn't think the time can be justified. But regardless of the size of the portfolio, it is vital to take the time with the client to collect the necessary information. If the portfolio is too small to invest time in, the better option is to not accept the prospect as a client. It is exactly these smaller portfolios that can and do lead to complaints.

With the availability of discount brokerage accounts and robo-advisors, full-service advisors can choose to reduce their risk by suggesting that clients with smaller accounts use those less expensive alternatives. Clients who don't want to spend the necessary time to enable the advisor to collect the needed information also have that option. But in any full-service advisor scenario, for both the client and the advisor, spending less time together is not an option. Here are some important things you need time for.

A. Take the time to find out important information about the client

It is crucial to spend sufficient time to allow you to get to know the client, including their values, financial situation, time horizon, risk profile, and other KYC issues, and to assess the client's goals and expectations. Having this information can ensure you make the right recommendations for the client.[1]

B. Take the time to explain the process to the client

It is also necessary to allow sufficient time together to permit you to properly explain to the client what the client should expect concerning the services, products, fees, and all the other issues that are involved in a client-advisor relationship.

You may be familiar with a TV show called *Marketplace*. The show, which seeks to protect consumers, featured an episode in which people were sent in with hidden cameras to meet with advisors seeking to invest their money.[2] The advisors and dealers, including some that were bank-owned, did not look good at all. In response to this episode, regulators did their own marketplace study and issued a joint report by the Ontario Securities Commission (OSC), the Investment Industry Regulatory Organization of Canada (IIROC), and the Mutual Fund Dealers Association of Canada (MFDA).[3] The OSC and self-regulatory organizations (SROS)[4] also sent

---

1   See *Advisor at Risk*, Chapters 3 and 4.

2   CBC *Marketplace* episode, "Hidden camera investigation uncovers 'atrocious' investment advice," aired February 28, 2014.

3   See "Mystery shopping for investment advice: Insights into advisory practices and the investor experience in Ontario," September 17, 2015, contained in OSC Staff Notice 31-715, IIROC Notice Number 15-0210, and MFDA Bulletin #0658-C.

4   Both IIROC and the MFDA are SROs.

mystery shoppers into the offices of several exempt market dealers (EMDs), investment dealers, mutual fund dealers, and portfolio managers to assess the client experiences and evaluate the quality of the investment advisory process. A 96-page report was issued, with, in my opinion, the most important information hidden at the back, in Appendix E. This appendix provides a guide for advisors to follow for their first meetings with clients so they will be in accordance with regulator and SRO expectations. I urge you to read Appendix E carefully and ask yourself whether you meet the best practices requirements. If not, you may have some work to do, particularly if your processes are more aligned with the category in the table described as noncompliant. Note how much more detail is expected by the regulators than just working through a KYC form. The information is relevant regardless of how you are registered or which province you live in.[5]

C. Take the time to enable the client to become both engaged in the process and sufficiently comfortable to ask questions

Clients may not realize that they need to devote sufficient time with their advisors to explore and ultimately land on what their goals are and how those goals might be achieved.[6] Advisors need to help clients understand that their engagement in the process is mandatory; it is the clients' money, and if they want to meet their own financial goals, they need to make managing it a priority.

---

5   See also *Advisor at Risk*, Chapter 3, specifically pages 50–56, for a detailed review of how to ensure you follow a KYC process.

6   This is the reason I have written the guide for clients that appears in the back of this book and is available for download online.

If a client or an advisor rushes through a meeting, the client will not have time to ask questions. The rushed client may not even digest the imparted information enough to be able to think of the questions they should ask. In many cases, clients may not feel comfortable asking questions, and may need time to warm up. Silence is not an indicator of understanding. In fact, asking relevant questions is a sign that the client understands the process and is engaged in it.

If more sophisticated clients need time to digest and consider questions, less sophisticated clients may need even more time. If a client doesn't ask any questions, you will need to figure out why. Is it a time constraint? A lack of engagement? Or does the client simply not understand what you have said sufficiently enough to even think of what questions they should ask?

D. Don't rush, even if you are running out of time

If you or the client are short of time, it is better not to rush. Simply suggest that the meeting be continued on another day. Advisors may be loath to do this, because it can feel like good service to work within the client's schedule and limited availably. But giving the relationship less time than it needs is not good service.

The advisor needs to show the client, by taking the time necessary to review matters in detail, that the client's money—and how best to invest it—are important to both client and advisor. Rushing through meetings will likely lead to the advisor not covering matters in sufficient detail, which can lead to major risks on both sides. Time is required for advisors both to protect their clients from getting unsuitable advice based on incomplete information, and to protect themselves from rushed and possibly incomplete paperwork that could come back to haunt them.

II. Clients Can Be Secretive, and Advisors Can Let Them Get Away with It

If a client is reluctant to share information and you choose to let them define those terms in your relationship, you are putting yourself at risk. Here are some strategies you can employ to get them to open up, or to protect yourself if they will not.

A. Assess each prospective client

If a prospective client seems secretive, make sure you are comfortable with the risk of taking on such a client. It is entirely about your own risk tolerance. Can you sleep at night knowing that you have likely breached many of the compliance requirements by opening an account and managing it without information that you need? Instead of having only one initial meeting, like with the Mr. Mookey example, I suggest you meet with prospects at least a couple of times before deciding to accept them as a client. It is much easier to refuse a prospect than to get a client to take their business elsewhere after an account is opened.[7]

Meet with the prospect more than once and see if they are willing to be more transparent as time goes on. Through several meetings, a client may become more open, and an advisor may be able to extract additional information and get a more reliable picture. This is the only way that the advisor can prove that they knew the client and was able to properly determine the client's risk profile and make appropriate recommendations. Be objective: if the prospect does not share enough information to enable you to test broad statements (like: "I

---

7   See *Advisor at Risk*, Chapter 7, page 112.

am a high-risk investor, all the way!"), or simply refuses to
share the information required, then I recommend that you do
not accept the prospect as a client.

B. Suggest a test drive if the prospect is secretive

Assuming you think the prospect could change over time,
try suggesting a "test drive": that is, suggest that the client
give you only a portion of their assets. Assuming the sum is
enough to diversify the account, the advisor can work with
the client for a period of time, getting to know each other better before the client sends the balance of the assets. (Set a
reasonable period at the beginning of the relationship.) Often,
the advisor is eager to get the assets transferred entirely and
immediately. But with a trial period, both client and advisor
can evaluate whether they can trust each other sufficiently to
continue working together. Just the offer to accept only part
of the assets, when a client is offering all of them, might give
that client the message that their advisor is not greedy and
that they are trustworthy. Furthermore, if the client continues to be secretive, the advisor will know that more time is
needed. It is better to take enough time to assess and get to
know the client than to rush into a relationship that will be
disappointing over time and that could lead to a stressful, and
possibly litigious, conclusion. If a client is high-maintenance
and continues to be secretive, then you may not want to continue with them at all, because it would not be a good use of
your time and resources.

C. Allow a secretive prospect to speak to your references

The prospect may be secretive because they do not know the
advisor. In this situation, you as the advisor may want to offer

them an opportunity to speak to clients who have come to trust you and share personal information with you. Refer prospective clients to existing clients with similar backgrounds to the prospect. For example, if this is a middle-aged, high-net-worth professional, choose references who are also middle-aged, high-net-worth professionals. This is a chance for advisors to distinguish themselves and explain how far they will go to be professional in every aspect of their business. Advisors may also suggest that prospective clients check their registration with the SRO or the securities regulator with which they are licensed. This way, the prospect can become satisfied that the advisor is trustworthy.

D. Probe into any areas that a client is secretive about

This is a necessary step for both prospects and existing clients who may be secretive. Ask questions about the specific issue they are hiding, and use different approaches or methods until you get the information you need. You can try to probe using indirect methods, more direct methods, very direct methods, and ultimately, if necessary, aggressive approaches.

For example, a client who is secretive about their income when talking to their advisor could be asked about the different sources of income they have and how they came to have them as a matter of interest. That would be less direct. After trying approaches like this to no avail, the advisor could resort to simply telling the client that they cannot choose the best investments for them without more information—becoming very direct. Or an advisor might be extremely direct, or even aggressive, by telling the prospective client that the advisor's relationship with their clients is based on the necessary transparency. If the client is not comfortable with the advisor, then perhaps, the advisor could say, they would be better served by someone else.

While I am not a communications expert, and a psychologist or social worker could give you a more effective approach than I could, I have had to extract information from my own clients who are secretive and perhaps ashamed. For example, one of my clients might believe that if they don't tell me about the skeleton in the closet, it might never be revealed in the litigation or regulatory matter. So I have to probe in different manners to extract such information. There have also been many cases in which, while cross-examining opposing parties, I have needed to approach the person in different ways to extract admissions that they would prefer I did not know.

I have found that a soft but direct approach can work: merely asking questions in a nonthreatening way. You can imagine that, as a litigation lawyer, my idea of nonthreatening will be very different from yours. But if the soft approach doesn't work, I then explain in a more direct manner the serious risks that could occur if the information is not imparted. I always say that this is about the clients, about meeting their needs and avoiding potential risks to them, as opposed to being about how I need this information to do my job (though it is both).

Here is an example of how you might use a soft but direct approach.

"Dr. Fruit, while I would very much like to have you as a client, I can't help feeling that you are not sufficiently comfortable with me. You are not giving me the information I need to ensure my advice is well suited to your situation. Is there something I can do to reassure you?"

If the softer approach doesn't work, try a more direct method.

"Dr. Fruit, while I would very much like to have you as a client, how can I help you meet your goals if I don't have the necessary information? The risk to you is that the plan we draw up for you and the investments we recommend won't be as good a fit as they should be because I am missing some information. I cannot let you take that risk."

Of course, if this is a high-net-worth client, as is commonly the case in these situations, the advisor would be very reluctant to send them away. However, advisors need to protect their license. Remember, it is the high-net-worth clients who have the resources to sue.

E. Alleviate the client's privacy concerns

If a client is reluctant to share information, it may be because they are worried about a breach of privacy. For this reason, it's good to be direct and ask such a client if their attitude toward sharing information is due to a previous negative experience with a professional. If this is the case, share with the client your privacy obligations, as well as the obligations of the company you are registered with. Tell the client the methods by which their information will be protected internally and on your software system at your office.

F. Find out if the client is afraid you will press them to hand over other assets

A secretive prospective client may be concerned that if the advisor knows about the client's other assets, they will pressure the client to transfer them. This is another good time to be direct and to ask outright if the client has this concern. If it is the case, assure the client that this will not happen—and make sure it doesn't.

G. Find out if the client has a general mistrust of advisors

To find out if this is the case with an existing or prospective client, ask more questions. A good one to start with is: "Why are you mistrustful of advisors?" Ask open-ended questions (for example, "What is it that concerns you about sharing your personal information with me?"), and challenge any negative opinions the client might express. If the client cannot be reasoned with, the advisor can reevaluate whether they want the client.

H. Are you taking on a secretive client?

If you intend to take on the secretive client, I offer two pieces of advice:

1. Err on the side of lower-risk investments, rather than higher, until you know the client well enough to be confident that they can take on more risk. If the client requests high-risk investments, you will be able to evaluate what they mean as you get to know them better. Further, as you get to know the client better, you can assess the client's financial position sufficiently to know if the client can afford to take the risk.

2. Whatever you do, don't rush a secretive prospect to become more open too quickly. Make it clear to the prospect or client that you are not in any rush to get the assets moved over. Be content to wait until clients or prospects trust you sufficiently to give you the information you need to make the relationship a success. This is an exercise you might be reluctant to follow because you think that if you don't get the assets transferred while the client is prepared to retain you, then you will lose an opportunity. Consider the risk and whether you can take it on and still sleep at night.

III. The Client Doesn't Understand Investments. and Is Seeking to Shift All Responsibility to the Advisor

Here is something I have learned about someone not understanding enough about a topic to ask an intelligent question—and I learned it from an issue I had with my car. I don't understand anything about cars. I cannot even figure out the right questions to ask when something goes wrong with my car. I took my car to the service center because the engine light was on. The necessary tests were performed and the mechanic told me that the computer didn't indicate anything was wrong, but the gas cap may have been loose, which may have triggered the engine light to go on. The light was now off, so I was told to return if the light went on again. Of course, this visit cost me a few bucks. As I drove away, I called my brother to tell him what was going on because he knows about cars. My brother asked me whether I had asked certain questions, which he listed without missing a beat. Why didn't I think of these questions? Cars are not intuitive or interesting to me and I was in a rush to get back to work. The light was off, I was on my way.

This experience gave me a better understanding of how clients feel when they meet with their advisors. The clients are busy and many might not know enough or be sufficiently interested in the subject matter of investing to even ask a question.

Is it the service center's obligation to explain matters clearly and educate me about cars? I don't know, but we do know it is the advisor's responsibility to ensure the client understands the strategy and the investments. However, something else struck me about my car experience. If the mechanic had slowed me down sufficiently enough to teach me something about cars, I might have appreciated his work and maybe even trusted him more. Instead, I wondered why he didn't check the gas cap first, before he hooked my car up to the monitor only to find nothing wrong. After all, it would have saved me the cost of the test.

Like with my lack of interest in cars,[8] many people do not have a natural interest in finances and investing. Like I did with my mechanic, clients seem to want to blindly hand their money over to an advisor and hope for the best, not spending the time to educate themselves. Advisors would benefit from determining the extent of their client's interest. If the answer is little or none, it's time to discuss their goals and expectations, rather than money and finance. Even if they are not interested in the latter, I expect they will be interested in the former.

I met with a successful advisor many years ago, and asked her how she engages her clients. She told me that her discussions with clients do not focus on the numbers or results, but instead focus on client goals, picking a different goal to discuss at each meeting. In this way, she gains a deep understanding of each client, and can choose topics important to that client in advance of each meeting.

If a client has little or no interest in finance, take the approach of this successful advisor. Rather than focusing exclusively on money and financial results, talk about their goals and expectations. This way, you can gain a deeper understanding of each client every time you meet with them, and perhaps engage them by focusing on what their investments can ultimately do for them.

---

8   I have since forced myself to learn more—I went to the car show this year!

Summary

There are a number of strategies advisors can employ at the outset of the advisor-client relationship to draw out secretive or disengaged clients and avoid the problems that result from communication breakdown. It is critical, at this early stage, to ensure that you acquire the information necessary—before you begin to manage the account. Spending enough time with each client is essential, so that the client feels sufficiently comfortable to share personal information and ask questions.

Advisors Take Action

✓ Meet with prospective clients several times to extract information and get a more reliable picture before deciding to accept them as a client. If a prospect is secretive, make sure you are comfortable with the risk of taking on such a client.

✓ Don't accept prospective clients who do not share the information necessary to enable you to properly assess their risk profiles and make appropriate investment recommendations.

✓ Ask questions to probe into areas your client is secretive about; if a softer approach doesn't work, try a more direct method. It may also be effective to accept only a small portion of a secretive client's assets on a "test drive" basis, so that you and the client can evaluate whether a relationship of trust can be built.

✓ Spend the time necessary with each client to collect the information you need, explain the process and what they should expect, and allow the client to become engaged and ask questions.

✓ Ask yourself whether your first meetings with clients meet the best practices expectations of the regulators and SROs.

✓ Determine the extent of your clients' interest in and understanding of finances and investing.

✓ Ensure that you focus on client goals and expectations in meetings.

3

Know Yourself

THIS CHAPTER WILL explain why you need to understand
yourself, your business, your dealer, and your regulator so
that you can develop a clear message to clients and fulfill
all dealer and regulatory requirements. With a clear message
to clients and a better understanding of your obligations, you
will be able to improve your communication with clients, fulfill
your compliance obligations, and limit the risk of infractions
and client complaints.

We'll also explore what you need to know about yourself, as
a professional advisor,[1] to avoid problems and succeed in this
industry. Let me explain with an example: Smee has been an
advisor, IIROC licensed, for more than 15 years. Five years ago,
Smee became licensed to sell insurance, and two years ago he

---

1   See also *Advisor at Risk*: the entirety of Chapter 2 is devoted to the subject of advisor
    as professional.

added a financial planning designation. This is what his dealer encouraged him to do. Smee is an entrepreneur. He is great with clients but not great with paperwork. Smee is confused because the more credentials he obtains, thereby increasing his service offering, the less money he makes. Smee wants to offer securities, insurance products, and financial planning to his clients, as he believes everyone needs all of these services. In order to offer these additional services, Smee is working longer hours, but he is still making less money.

Smee blames his lack of profitability on new regulations that require more forms, more signatures, and more correspondence. He also blames his dealer's red tape, which is stressing him out. Smee is spending more time than ever before getting documents signed, initialed, and signed again by clients, and he is exhausted! Apparently, there have been compliance problems in the branch and the dealer was clamping down, which was adding to his stress. One of the advisors was hauled in by the branch manager after an audit because the auditors noted that there was not enough detail in the advisor's electronic notes of client meetings, and forms were missing. That advisor had been threatened with dismissal if he didn't improve substantially. He also has a record with the regulator, as he had been penalized for his sloppiness, which was publicized on the internet in a settlement agreement entered into with the regulator.

Smee is losing sleep worrying that he will be the next to be hauled in because he isn't great with paperwork. He knows that he is at risk. He needs to stop and examine himself and his business.

I. Advisors Benefit from Knowing Themselves

While an advisor may have many qualifications, like Smee, they may need to be more focused. To accomplish this, advisors need to know their strengths and weaknesses, which products and services they are prepared to offer (and which they are not), and to be honest with themselves about how much compliance risk they are prepared to take on.

Advisors also need to know the limits of what they can and cannot do for clients. Limitations may be self-imposed, due to what they don't want to do, or find too risky to do. Limitations may also be imposed by external forces, like legal or regulatory restrictions. Advisors will be unable to communicate clearly to clients until they understand their strengths and weaknesses and the restrictions on the services they are permitted to provide to clients.

I have taught thousands of advisors across Canada, and when I discuss the topic of knowing themselves in this manner, it mostly falls on deaf ears. These advisors were not rookies. Many had more than one license; some were accountants. Some had financial planning designations, as well as certifications to be portfolio managers and insurance agents. What they had in common was their inability to clearly and succinctly articulate who they were and what services and value they offered. Yet understanding this is necessary to succeed in the financial services industry.

A. Consider your strengths and weaknesses, likes and dislikes

Just because you dislike doing something, it doesn't mean you are not good at it. The opposite may be true as well. For example, you may hate paperwork, but you might actually be good at doing it because of your attention to detail. Conversely, and this is just an example, you may love researching and picking stocks yourself, but this may be very time-consuming. Others assigned this task may be better at this component.

Try this important exercise. Take a moment to have a brainstorming session, in which you write down your strengths and weaknesses, likes and dislikes. For each question, whether you answer "yes" or "no," ask yourself whether you are particularly good at the task, regardless of whether you like or dislike it. While I offer you the following chart, it is really just a tool to help you begin your own brainstorming; it is not meant to be a comprehensive list. Spend some time thinking about all the tasks you do in your work, and design your own list around that.

Prospecting	Good at it?	Like it?
Cold calling		
First meeting with prospects		
Developing a personal connection with prospects/clients		

Clients	Good at it?	Like it?
Staying connected with clients		
Obtaining personal/private information from clients		

Connecting with the following age groups to obtain personal information and develop rapport	Good at it?	Like it?
< 30		
31–45		
46–60		
61–70		
> 71		
Also consider religious, cultural, language, ethnic, or other backgrounds		

Servicing	Good at it?	Like it?
Couples		
Families		
Complex trust and succession accounts		
Institutions		

Tasks	Good at it?	Like it?
Researching companies/products		
Planning—developing/updating plans		
Portfolio development		
Portfolio rebalancing		
Economic analysis		
Prospectus review		
Analyst reports review		

Let's look at how Smee would answer these questions, and how his responses could help him improve.

Smee's analysis would be like this:

SMEE'S STRENGTHS

- Connects well with people, regardless of age, gender, etc.
- Is credible, honest, and trustworthy, which clients appreciate and therefore they trust him
- Is able to get personal information from clients because they trust him
- Is great with numbers and concepts; very smart but does not like to do research because he doesn't have the time
- Is patient and excellent at explaining products to clients; understands the products well, regardless of complexity
- Is approachable and clients feel comfortable asking him questions

SMEE'S WEAKNESSES

- Never seems to have enough time to collect information from clients; schedules meetings too close together; often forced to schedule follow-up meetings to complete what is necessary
- Doesn't do a thorough analysis of clients' risk profiles or objectives
- Rushes through the preparation of clients' financial plans, since he doesn't like doing them
- Poor note-taking

IF YOU TAKE all these answers together and analyze Smee's practice, it would seem that he:

a. has a time management problem;
b. needs better processes in place;
c. is great with people and great at getting new clients but needs focus in choosing a target market;
d. needs an experienced assistant who can help him with scheduling and paperwork;
e. would benefit from delegating the preparation of financial plans;
f. would function better with fewer clients, working harder with each to drill down on risk profiles and objectives;
g. needs to install processes to ensure he is operating in a compliant fashion with follow-up and note-taking; and
h. needs to schedule enough time for meetings to get everything done without requiring a follow-up meeting.

SMEE IS OPERATING a risky business. If he doesn't change and focus on these problems, he will likely run into trouble with his clients, his dealer, or the regulator because of service and paperwork deficiencies, or worse. No wonder he is losing sleep.

After you create your own task chart and review the questions in it, using it as a guide to better understand your strengths and weaknesses and likes and dislikes, you will be able to determine what services to offer, to whom, and how. You can examine the answers and choose deliverables in a manner that benefits you and your clients.

I have done this exercise for myself, using questions that were relevant to my profession. It was this exercise that led me to understand that I needed to shift my model by moving from a big law firm with a big overhead to a smaller firm with a smaller overhead, so that I could reduce my hourly rate and get more work from the financial industry. Having the team I wanted was also very important to me, and that meant I had to move. It was only through this analysis that I was able to figure out how to change the model around me to meet my needs, and my clients' needs. Now that my business model is right, I can focus on offering clients what I do best and enjoy the most.

After you complete your chart and your analysis, then, like me, consider the elements surrounding you. Do your values and business plan align with your dealer/MGA? Do you have the right team to provide the products and services that you want to provide? Then consider whether you should make a change.[2]

Once you've made any changes you need to make, you can focus your deliverables and delegate to team members or outside referrals, whose skills complement your offerings. You will be more efficient and focused, and likely happier and more fulfilled. You will be able to explain to clients your services in a clearer and more efficient manner, and more easily choose clients who need your core services and products.

B. Consider your risk tolerance

Another important step is to determine how much risk you can tolerate in your business to ensure you can sleep at night.

Risk tolerance usually pertains to clients, so you might wonder why I am using it to refer to advisors. Indeed, I am turning 'risk tolerance' on its head because I am challenging you to determine your own risk tolerance, not in the context of investment risk but rather of business risk: risk to your license, reputation, and livelihood. This risk comes from client complaints, compliance infractions, or regulatory risk. To explain, let's look at two extreme examples.

---

2   If you have an investigation pending by either the dealer or your regulator, discuss with your lawyer before considering any potential move as your license transfer could be delayed in these circumstances.

The most risk-averse advisor

If you are in this category, you cannot tolerate any risk whatsoever. You always want to reduce your risk by being thorough and careful with every document and every client meeting. You take detailed notes of every meeting, and later transcribe (or copy/scan) them into your software system. You take your time and incorporate processes that ensure you are absolutely compliant. You apply a standard of perfection. If anything goes even slightly wrong with any documents, you will lose sleep until a new system is established to resolve this problem.

The least risk-averse advisor

If you fall into this category, you focus only on growing your business, since you can tolerate the threat of a client complaint or regulatory investigation. Likely, you choose not to "waste time" ensuring forms or paper trails of communication with clients are properly maintained. You are not concerned; you think it will all take care of itself, delegating all compliance tasks to others—for example, junior advisors or assistants. Your supervisor returns all incomplete documents, and it is your assistant who sends these back to clients to complete.[3] If your assistant cuts some corners, that is for the benefit of efficiency for clients, so you think that's okay. You sleep well and you don't sweat the small stuff.

MOST ADVISORS OPERATE somewhere in between these two extremes. However, advisors are usually unaware of the risks

---

3   Note that at the time of writing, the MFDA has imposed significant reporting requirements on MFDA dealers concerning problems with forms, including incomplete, pre-signed, and falsification of signatures. Many of these matters led to investigations and settlements publicized on the internet.

they take; if and when these advisors are approached by their dealer or regulator with compliance concerns, they are often surprised.

In the example of Smee, he has been operating with a significant amount of risk in his business, both regulatory and legal, because he doesn't have proper processes in place. While he is stressed out, he cannot even identify or articulate the risks he is taking or the problems that could arise. Most advisors can't.

Through the years, several advisors have approached me to ask if I would come to their office and risk-proof their business. I developed a program called a process review, whereby I reviewed their paperwork and processes and made suggestions for improvement. I developed a questionnaire for advisors to complete in advance so I could learn about their business, and I would follow this with an office visit to meet with the advisor and their staff and review a sample file or two. Then I would give them feedback for improvement.

Through this exercise, I came to realize that even those advisors who expressed an interest in and were willing to pay for this exercise were still reluctant to change to reduce their risk. They were really only interested in getting a positive report card from me. If I didn't simply confirm that they were doing it all properly, they lost interest.

One such advisor who hired me to risk-proof his business had bragged, in advance of hiring me, that his office operated with several processes and was completely compliant. He specifically described to me several great note-taking processes he had implemented. I went to his office and looked at a couple of files. They were a mess! I asked for the notes of discussions during client meetings, as he had told me this was a process he followed. But his assistant told me there were no notes, hard copy, electronic, or otherwise. When I reviewed with him what

I thought about his file organization and compliance risk, he told me he would sort this out in our next meeting. But he canceled, so that meeting never happened. This was a recurring theme with many clients. Too many advisors were prepared to pay me to review their business, so long as I didn't report anything deficient.

This particular type of advisor seems to have no interest in identifying where the risk in their business exists, and no interest in changing their processes to deal with risk. They prefer instead to continue to operate as they had before. That is, until they find themselves in my office seeking legal representation, when suddenly they are extremely distraught. If only they had seen it coming.

Most of the advisors who retain me on regulatory or legal compliance infractions, or to respond to client complaints, say they never saw it coming. When I review their files, it is clear that there were several alarm bells ringing that, had they been heeded, would have allowed them to head off potential problems before they arose. It was clear from a review of the files that there was a lack of communication and organized paperwork, and that the notes were inadequate.

It is one thing to decide to operate in a noncompliant and risky manner; it is another thing to not be aware of it. Taking on risk should be a decision, and that decision should be based on the advisor's risk tolerance. Do you depend on this business for the financial support of yourself and your loved ones? Are you the type to be horrified with the public circulation on the web of a regulatory infraction? Do you have a readily available Plan B? For example, could your family get by on your spouse's income if your license was threatened?

Advisors who conduct their business with a significant amount of risk either practice what I call the "ostrich phenomenon," sticking their head in a hole, remaining unaware, and hoping for the best,[4] or they might be aware of the risks but have a high risk tolerance.

My advice is: know your risk tolerance, be honest with yourself about the risk in your business, and operate according to the amount of risk you can tolerate. This will help you decide two things:

1. Who you choose as a client and who you send away.[5] "I am sorry, Dr. Fruit, but I think you should try to sort it out with your existing advisor [the fourth advisor for Dr. Fruit in the past 10 years] instead of jumping to another one."

2. What to communicate to clients, especially when they ask you to cut corners for them. A client asks their advisor: "Can you just sign that form for me this one time as it is inconvenient to get it signed?"; or the client says to their advisor: "Just buy what you think is right for me as I don't need to be bothered with your telephone calls."[6]

Knowing your own risk profile will enable you to identify risks that exceed your tolerance, understand why something is noncompliant, and communicate a clear message to your prospective and existing clients that you will not proceed in a manner that exposes you and your business to risk beyond what you can tolerate.

---

4   These advisors suffer a huge amount of stress and have many sleepless nights.
5   For a detailed discussion of types of problem clients, see *Advisor at Risk*, Chapter 7.
6   This example assumes the advisor is not a portfolio manager.

II. Advisors Benefit from Knowing Their Business

Once an advisor can articulate what they are and what they are not, they can do the fun part—evaluate and, perhaps, rebuild or rework their business into something better aligned with themselves. They can grow a more focused business that reflects their strengths, weaknesses, and risk tolerance.

Building a business is like building a house. You can build the most spectacular house, but if the foundation is not solid, the house will always have problems. Building a strong foundation begins with the right business plan. A strong and clear business plan permits an advisor to communicate a consistent and clear message. This message helps manage clients' expectations about what they will do and what they will not, what they will sell and what they will not, what the fee will be, and what the client will get for that fee.

A. Licenses and certifications

Based on the licenses and certifications you and others have in your team, branch, or dealer, you will want to decide what services and products will be offered, within the parameters of what is permitted by each regulator. Knowing those parameters is crucial to ensuring that you and others do not overstep the boundaries of your licenses and certifications.

While you may have more than one license or certification, the determination from the previous section on knowing yourself should assist you in deciding which license you want to use to sell which products, and which tasks you want to delegate to others or refer to someone outside your team.[7] You

---

7   If you accept or pay a referral fee, be certain that it is consistent with the laws and regulations associated with your license or certificate.

want to be disciplined in your approach, rather than trying to be all things to all people.

When considering what services and products to sell, and which to refer to others, you will decide based on your license(s) and what is better for your clients. You will also want to consider what is profitable for you and your team. While educating yourself and obtaining different certifications is terrific, you could find that you are spreading yourself too thin. This may not be practical or profitable, and you may find that you are not focusing your business effectively. Growing a business is not the only issue; growing it in a compliant, efficient, and profitable manner is key.

B. Target market

Let us say you used the exercise in the previous section to determine your preferred target market. Now you want to analyze your current business to determine who your clients are and in which categories they fit. You will need to take an inventory and do an analysis. Are they of all ages, backgrounds, and socio-economic levels? Or are they more narrow in scope? Is your current client base consistent with your preferences and the type of clients you connect with the best?

It is also important to analyze client turnover. It is costly to have a business in which there is a high turnover, so if that is the case, consider the reasons. It is not a bad thing if clients leave because your business is more focused and they don't fit your target, or if they were too high maintenance. While it is best to have a consistent, solid client base, analyze the clients you lost and consider whether or not you would have liked to keep them.

When you are meeting a prospective client, ask yourself: Does this prospect fit my target in terms of age, socio-economic background, and education? Do they want the type of services

I offer? Or would they be better off with something outside my realm of expertise?

If a prospect calls me for litigation that is within my area of expertise—securities litigation, regulatory matters, employment litigation—then I am pleased to take the client. However if it is in an area that I know one of my partners has particular expertise, I will refer the client to them. If a prospect calls me for advice in an area that is outside of our office's expertise, like personal injury or family law, I will refer them to another lawyer who is expert in that area, usually providing three names and encouraging them to do their own due diligence.[8] I am focused on my area of expertise and what I love to do. I know my target market is advisors and dealers in the financial services industry (including insurance products like segregated funds and life insurance), so that is where I direct all my energy and effort.

Once you determine what type of clients you would like to target, you need to become an expert in that area and appreciate the unique characteristics and issues facing these clients. For example, if your target clients are professional women,[9] you will need to educate yourself about what financial issues professional women are facing. Beware of generalizations: no group is homogeneous, so be careful not to paint all people in a group with a single brush. Be open and flexible.

Even if you are in the same category as the target you choose—for example, you target professional women and you are a professional woman—be sure not to generalize based on your own experience. Your potential clients might be very different from you. Be sure also to communicate to them in a manner that is sensitive to their culture, age, and background.

---

8   Lawyers practicing in Ontario can charge referral fees, but I do not.
9   See Chapter 8 for more on women clients.

C. Your place or mine?

Has your business required you to travel for hours to see clients at a location convenient for them? Do you live in a rural area in which the population of potential clients is too limited, or are there so many advisors servicing a small area that you need to go farther? Consider whether you want to limit your visits only to clients who are profitable for you. If you are spending more on gas and wear and tear on your car, and you find these long drives stressful, then it may be time to reconsider.

Determine your boundaries[10] and communicate to prospects that you are unable to accept them as clients due to the travel distance. If they choose to travel to your office, then communicate this orally and in writing so that they don't later complain that you don't come to see them at their home. Putting it in writing serves to both manage their expectations and to remind clients who may later forget. It is something concrete you can refer them to later.[11]

Some advisors, however, may consider something like this to be a differentiating factor that attracts clients and doesn't wear on them too much. For example, even though I work in downtown Toronto, where there are hundreds of advisors, my advisor lives and works over an hour's drive from my office and home. While I am sure my advisor doesn't drive to every one of her clients' homes or offices, she and I take turns traveling—sometimes I don't mind driving to her office (especially since she lets my dog come, too!), and other times she comes

---

10 This can also serve as a metaphor for determining your boundaries in all aspects of your business: stay focused and communicate these boundaries to prospects and clients.

11 Putting any term in writing will also serve this dual purpose. It effectively becomes a term of the agreement that you can refer back to later, if the client gives you a hard time.

to my home or office. When I chose this advisor, we discussed this issue and she told me she would make it easy for me, traveling to my office at least once a year.

D. Services rendered

Though your core business might be buying and selling securities or insurance, you may offer other services, some for which you charge and some that may be loss leaders. Regardless of whether you charge for these services or not, you need to ensure you remain expert in the area. Ask yourself if you are able to stay on top of more than one type of product or service. If not, you might need help from another licensed person who has more expertise in that area.

Here is an example: Gooshow, an advisor, has her CFP (certified financial planner) designation and feels strongly that all her clients should have a financial plan. But preparing the plan is very time-consuming. Gooshow works for a dealer that employs financial planners specifically (and only) to prepare plans for clients. While Gooshow is perfectly qualified and really enjoys the exercise of preparing her clients' financial plans, she is spreading herself too thin. She is not able to do the plans as thoroughly and thoughtfully as she should. Therefore, she finds it more productive and profitable—and less risky to her business—to focus on her core offering of securities, and to delegate the planning to another person.

Of course, Gooshow will explain to clients that while she delegates the preparation of the financial plans, the service will be seamless as far as the client is concerned. This reassures clients that they will be well taken care of. Communicating this to clients is important so they know who is doing what and why.

I am transparent in my practice. When I delegate to my associates or partners, I explain to my clients why this is in their interest: it could be less expensive, more efficient, or both! Transparency is also reflected in my invoices, in which I provide the name of the person who completed each task, a detailed description of the task, how much time it took, and the hourly rate. I don't want my clients to be surprised or to feel that because my associate is doing some of the heavy lifting, I am not giving the matter sufficient attention. I explain that I review all of my associate's work and we develop the strategy together. Usually it is teamwork: I lead the team and my associates and client are on the team, and my assistant keeps us organized!

E. Fee-based or commission?

Are you offering your services on a fee-based model, a commission basis, or both?[12] On what basis are you making this decision? Is it for the benefit of the clients or for your own benefit? You need to be clear to clients how you are charging them. Ensure that if you offer both models, the one chosen is the better one for the particular client.

You are obliged, if you are offering both payment models, to explain to the client in a transparent manner the pros and cons of each model. If you explain that the fee-based model offers the client more services than the commission model, in which each service is an extra charge, make sure that you are actually charging in the manner you are describing. For example, if you tell clients that financial plans are included in the fee-based model but are extra in the commission model, then that needs to be true—not just because it would be frowned upon by the regulator if you misled a client but also because it would be unprofessional to lure clients into using a fee-based

---

12   Note that this book does not explore CRM or CRM2. I just encourage full transparency in all that you do, including cost to client.

model if it would be less expensive for them if they were charged a commission.

F. Team

Do you have the team to do it? What are the limits to your team? Do you need to hire or fire? If you intend to focus more on insurance, or securities, you will need to consider whether you want a licensed specialist to deal with clients in the other area of expertise.

Do the assistants working with you have the expertise and skills required for the team? In this business, assistants play a very important role and need to understand the business, have an excellent ability to attend to detail, and be good with clients. These qualities may be hard to find. So when you do find such a person, be certain that you keep them happy, because turnover in this position can hurt your business. This is especially true if your clients know and like your assistant and rely on them as much as you do.

Make sure that your team members understand their roles and follow up with regular meetings to ensure everyone is operating consistently when it comes to processes, compliance obligations, and what was promised to clients.

If a client or regulator is unhappy with any of the team members, each team member risks being included in any regulatory matter and/or litigation. Remember, any infraction committed by administrative staff is ultimately the advisor's responsibility, whether the staff member is licensed or not. The licensed administrative staff who committed the infraction and the advisor will likely both be held responsible by the regulator, dealer, and judge. As I always say, you are the company you keep, and that is absolutely the case when it comes to regulatory matters or litigation, because everyone on the team may be hauled in. Gauge the risk tolerance of your team members as well as your own, so that no one is operating at a risk level higher than yours.

III. Advisors Benefit from Defining Their Business

Once an advisor has completed the heavy lifting of getting to know themselves and their business (using the methods I outlined in sections I and II), the next part can be easier and a little more fun. This is where advisors get to define themselves and choose what they will do going forward, including deciding how many clients they want to take on, who they want to service, and what products they want to offer.

A. To change or not to change

You may need just a bit of refining or you may need to make some big changes. Either way, this exercise is crucial to your success, and is intended to improve your business and reduce your risk.

Your office may need to develop processes to choose the right clients, the right products, and the right services, and to follow up with clients regularly.

Your team members may need to develop processes for note taking and communication with clients and with one another. Regular meetings to improve and add processes, and to ensure they are being followed, are recommended. Continuing education on new compliance requirements is also advisable.

B. Build a clear, concise message and be consistent

Now that you have done the work to establish the focus of your business, the team, and its offerings, you are in a position to build a clear and concise message to communicate to clients in person, on your website, and in all of your marketing material. This message should be consistent with everything you do, and convey that you are transparent and have encouraged clients to make choices that are in their best interests.[13] This clear, concise message will give your clients confidence in you and your team.

C. Follow-through: Just do it! And charge for it!

You can build processes and manners of communication with clients that are designed to ensure they understand the value of the service and products you offer. If what you offer is presented in a clear fashion, and the value is there, they will be satisfied. It will be less about straight investment returns and more about the entire service, including the product offering and the trust they have in you to direct and advise them in a manner that is in their best interest.

Summary

The ability to clearly articulate who you are and what services and value you offer to clients is necessary to succeed in the financial services industry. All advisors need to understand themselves, their business, their dealer, and their regulator to develop a clear, consistent message to clients and fulfill all dealer and regulatory requirements.

---

13 When I use the language 'best interest' throughout this book, I do not suggest that is the legal standard at this point. While there is a strong push by some of the regulators to change the standard to a 'best interest' standard, this has not yet been passed at the time of this writing. What I mean by 'best interest' is that an advisor should, regardless of the legal standard, treat clients in a manner that looks out for their clients' best interests.

Advisors Take Action

✓ Know your strengths and weaknesses, and the restrictions on the services you are willing and permitted to provide to clients. Consider engaging in a brainstorming exercise to analyze your strengths and weaknesses, likes and dislikes, to determine what services to offer, to whom, and how.

✓ Know your risk profile, be honest with yourself about the risk in your business, and operate according to the amount of risk you can tolerate.

✓ Develop a business plan that allows you and your team to grow your business in a compliant, efficient, and profitable manner. Make sure that your team members understand their roles and follow up with regular meetings to ensure consistency.

✓ Once you know yourself, define your business by building a clear and concise message to communicate to clients—one that is transparent and consistent with everything you do.

4

Know Your Client

AFTER YOU HAVE looked inward and come to know yourself and your business, it is time to look outward to clients. This chapter will explore your communication with clients: how clear and consistent communication leads to success, and lack thereof leads to failure. We will also explore the key to building your business: listening to your clients.

I. Do You Want to Grow Your Business?

Knowing your client, and listening to your client, is the key to bridging the communication gap and building your business. Here's how to get started.

A. Building a strong foundation

Growing your business in this industry is a huge challenge. With threats from online robo-advisors and with cut-throat competition among advisors battling it out to get the wealthiest clients, the challenge is real.

The first step is to determine whether or not you have a strong business foundation on which to grow. By that, I mean: are you doing a great job with existing clients? If your foundation is not solid, then you are probably losing clients, likely due to failure to meet or surpass their expectations. If that is the case, focusing on building your business will be an exercise in futility. This is true for the following reasons:

1. *The revolving door.* If you focus on building your business before you have developed good processes and habits and strong communication with existing clients, then you will have a revolving door of existing clients leaving while new ones are coming in. Client referrals will be few, if any, and, worse, clients will be spreading bad news about you, rather than singing your praises. With the internet, word spreads fast. Trying to build your business from an unstable foundation is a bad use of your resources and not the recipe for success.

2. *Referrals.* A good way to grow your business is through referrals. The best way to get clients referred to you is by building strong relations with existing clients. That is, in part, what I mean by a strong foundation. This won't happen if your clients don't have good things to say about you.

3. *Client complaints.* If your existing clients are dissatisfied, then you risk receiving a client complaint. A single client complaint may become public and wreak havoc on your

reputation and confidence, which in turn will impact your ability to attract new clients.

4. ***Moving between dealers.*** A weak foundation leading to client complaints or poor compliance audit results can lead to the termination of your relationship with your sponsoring company. Each of the dealers must file documents with the regulator when you leave, so that the regulator knows you are no longer being sponsored by that company (along with the reason for your departure). If the company you are leaving reports compliance issues, this will likely lead to difficulties getting the regulator to move your license to another company. There could be a delay of months, or the regulator could flat-out refuse to allow you to be registered, given the concerns with your compliance record.

While growing your business, it is still important to protect your existing business. So how can you do both at the same time? By installing processes that ensure you exceed your clients' expectations. This pertains not just to returns on capital; it also means understanding and taking a genuine interest in your clients. You have heard of the importance of 'Know Your Client', but this is a different context. This is not just about ensuring you are compliant; this is about actually *understanding* your clients.

B. Servicing existing clients

Here is the proposition: if you do a great job for your existing clients, they will want you to succeed. What does doing a great job mean? Let's start with what it doesn't mean. The following is a list of the things some advisors do that are problematic and do not serve clients well:

- Talking too much at client meetings.
- Not listening to the client or asking enough questions.
- Not taking a genuine interest in client's financial and other successes, problems, and concerns.
- Rushing through paperwork and not asking if there have been any changes in the client's circumstances.
- Rushing through explanations without ascertaining whether or not the client understands.
- Not responding to the client in a timely and thoughtful manner.
- Rushing through telephone calls or meetings.
- Relying too much on generic emails instead of personalized correspondence.
- Relying on one-way (meaningless) communication like birthday cards or mass emails.
- Failing to follow up or follow through with promises made to the client.
- Relying too much on impersonal methods of communication and not scheduling enough face-to-face meetings.

An advisor operating in this manner will not succeed. There will be a breakdown in communication. Existing clients will feel neglected and there will be a greater risk of client complaints.

On the flip side is a recipe you can follow that will lead you to success:

- **Be a good listener.** Take a genuine interest in your clients. When they mention something personal, explore it. Be an active listener and encourage clear communication by drilling down into whatever concerns they are raising.

- **Give the clients the time they need.** If the client is trying to rush you, encourage them to slow down. Remind them that it is their money and they need to invest their time and energy to ensure you get it right.

- *Let go of clients you are unwilling or unable to service.* Instead of underservicing clients you consider too small to invest time in, send them to a different advisor.

- *Endeavor to solve your client's problems.* Go further than selling them what you sell everyone else, and instead sell them something they need and that is suitable. If the service you provide does not meet their needs, they will not stay with you and will not recommend you to their contacts. The only way to understand what people need is by listening to them.

- *Put your client's needs first.* Some services you provide might not make you money directly, but don't think it will go unnoticed. Being effective is all about helping your clients, whether it makes you money or not. The benefits will be obvious in the long run.

- *Keep up with client changes.* While you may have met the client's needs at the outset of the relationship, you may not have done so as the client's circumstances change.

- *Define the terms you use.* Ensure that your clients understand everything you say, like 'risk' and 'time horizon'. Clients generally nod their head, indicating they are following, but they are often just glazing over at these terms if they don't understand them and the terms are not clearly defined for them.

II. Understanding and Applying These Principles

The balance of this chapter will explain the importance of following these key principles: listening carefully to what clients say; taking time to understand their needs; solving problems for them; putting their needs first even if there is no immediate pay-off; and keeping up with changes in their lives.

A. The story of how I found my advisor

My own personal experience with advisors who have managed my portfolio is a good example of how these principles work. I had a great advisor managing my account when I was in the early years of my law practice. He was a portfolio manager. I remember in those first meetings how he told me that he would invest well for me, but he was not in the business of calling me in advance of the annual RRSP deadline or of offering any other type of service for that matter. He was strictly an investment guy. This was fine for me at the time. I stayed with him for several years; the returns were very good and I liked him.

After I had children, though, my needs changed. I needed an RESP and so I opened one with another advisor who was a friend of a friend. He was also very nice. The returns were fine. He never called me to discuss whether my education fund was sufficient and he never explained how the government grants worked or the free money I would miss out on if I didn't make regular contributions. I was getting older, as were my two children. I was beginning to worry about not having a plan for my retirement and my children's education. By this time, I was a partner in a law firm and these were my earning and saving years. I began to realize that I had better consider developing a plan. Was I saving enough? Did I take full advantage of the RESP government grants? Clearly, my needs were changing, and my advisors were not keeping up. I needed a new advisor, someone who would help me draw up a plan and implement it.

Given that I teach and represent advisors and had met thousands to that point in my life, finding a new one should have been easy. While I really didn't have anyone in mind, I knew what I wanted, and didn't want, in an advisor. I had a clear list. I liked the stocks that my portfolio manager had chosen and I was doing well, so I did not want to go into a managed account at a securities dealer. Rather, I needed someone to keep an eye on my stocks, and to help me stay on top of my personal financial situation (RRSP, RESP, mortgage, and all other financial decisions).

I asked around and received three names. I asked my assistant to contact each of them and arrange telephone interviews. My assistant arranged calls with two of the three. The third said he would prefer to meet me in person, and that he would make it convenient by coming to my office. I asked my assistant to call him back and tell him I was conducting telephone interviews only. She came back and told me he was insistent that we meet in person.

While one might say that meeting in person is a better way to interview a prospective client—and may even be a better way for me to interview him—my response was to remove him from the list. Harsh? Tough? Probably, but this is what struck me. He was not a good listener. The in-person meeting was what he wanted, not what I wanted. He was not listening to my simple request. He may have been the best advisor in the world, but if he couldn't adjust to my needs and request, then he was not for me.

I interviewed the second one by telephone. I was told that this advisor only did managed accounts.

And then there was one. The third advisor had one strike against her in that she was not conveniently located close to my office or home. I spoke to her by telephone and gave her my list of needs. She listened intently and confirmed that these needs could be met. She explained that she had a portfolio manager on her team and that she would work with him to choose the securities. She said she had children just a little older than mine and would help me navigate my RESPs. She told me she would make sure I had my investments properly managed. I also liked her reaction when I told her that I had been maximizing my RRSP contributions since age 20. She was so positive and encouraging. I liked that she had many years of experience. When I raised the issue of her office location, she assured me that she would come to me for meetings so this would not be a problem. The stars were aligned—I hired her!

Now, it is one thing to be a good listener and promise to deliver. It is altogether another matter to actually deliver. She has indeed delivered all that she promised. She comes to me unless I offer to go to her office, which I do from time to time. She developed a plan for me and continues to help me execute on it. I feel like I have a partner helping me with my financial needs, especially as those needs change. When I feel discouraged, she encourages me. When I worry, she finds out what is worrying me. She suggests adjustments to my plan and we put these into action. Why and how does she accomplish this? She knows me and understands me. She watches as I change and she adjusts for me.

It is not always to her financial benefit to do the things she does for me. For example, she knows how busy I am, so when it came time to renegotiate my mortgage, she told me to remain with the institution I was with, instead of switching to the institution she works for. She said the terms were better and, knowing how busy I am and how much I hate red tape, there would be less paperwork, since they were already the mortgagee for my property. That created goodwill. When I had savings beyond my RRSP contributions, instead of telling me to put it in my account with her firm, she knew the terms of my mortgage and directed me to make additional payments to my mortgagee (the bank). When I decided to leave Toronto's Bay Street and move my practice to my little firm on Front Street, we developed a plan to pay off my mortgage and have no personal debt when I left. This was totally consistent with my personal values and allowed me to sleep at night. I knew she was not making recommendations to benefit herself. Instead, she was suggesting what was best for me, her client.

If my advisor gives me advice that does not benefit her directly, or at least immediately, how can she get ahead? Put simply, I am a referral source. While my advisor will not get rich with my account, I have referred to her at least a handful of clients. Colleagues regularly ask me who they should use as an advisor. I tell them that I only have experience with my advisor, and I refer them to her and at least one other whom I do not have much experience with. Why do I refer clients to my advisor? Because I want to see her succeed, just like she wants me to succeed.

This explains how listening and keeping up-to-date with your clients' changes are crucial. It is also crucial to really understand what makes your clients tick and how this changes from time to time.

B. Understanding your clients—what makes them tick?

Every client is different and has their own special story. If you think of the people you know well, you know how and why they came to be the people they are today. To be an effective advisor, you need to understand your client's story. They must be willing to share it with you, and you need to listen and remember the story when it comes time to make recommendations.

My advisor knows my story. She needs to know it to understand my values. I hate debt and am a big saver. I am not materialistic, preferring simple rather than flashy or fancy. I am risk averse. Why? Because I have a riches-to-rags story. I grew up in a very affluent family. We had staff working in the house and servants' quarters in our four-story mansion. We went to private schools. We had a ski chalet and a membership in a yacht club, where my grandparents kept their 49-foot cruiser and my father kept his sailboat. My siblings and I went to expensive summer camps. I was accustomed to all of that. But when I was 12 years old, my father decided that he didn't like his life anymore and left my mother with four children. I was the youngest. He didn't just leave, he really left! He didn't want to pay support for us or my mother. He sold his business for a dollar and moved out of the jurisdiction so a court order compelling him to support us could not be enforced.[1] Before he left, he secured the house with a lien so my mother couldn't sell it to support us with the proceeds.

My mother was 40 years old and had never worked outside the home for a day in her life. She was in her early 20s when

---

1   While I have no expertise in the area of family law, inter-provincial laws may now exist to protect families in our situation.

she got married and had children, and she took care of managing the family. After my father left, she started to work, as did the rest of us. I was 12 years old when I got a job working five days a week after school and on weekends. By the time the lien was removed from our house by court order, I was 19 years old. We had lived hand-to-mouth for seven years in a huge house. I have never been unemployed since that time. While other people's stories may be much worse than mine, this experience had a lasting effect on my attitude toward money and finances.

This is the story that shapes me and affects every dollar that I spend and save. It affects my attitude toward having a career and being financially self-sufficient. Any advisor I work with needs to know this story, so they understand my needs and concerns and can help me make decisions from my point of view, with my values in mind.

So you see, understanding your client is far more than completing a KYC form. If you want long-term clients, the secret is in learning the backstory: knowing where they come from, and what their experiences have been, for better or for worse.

As an aside, when I transferred my investable assets from my previous advisor, he was really surprised. I found that shocking. I had told him that I needed more than an excellent stock jockey. I had said I needed a financial partner to help me with all aspects of my personal financial situation. He had told me that this was not part of his business. So I don't know why he was surprised that I moved my business to someone else.

C. Listen more; talk less

If you don't know your clients, you really cannot know how to help them. If all you are thinking is "How can I close this deal?" then you will not prosper. If your client isn't the focus of the relationship, or if you think you don't need to explore with clients who they are, where they come from, and how they feel as a result, then I don't think you're following a recipe for success.[2]

Many advisors complain that clients are not open with them, which precludes them from gathering the information required by law and regulation. Clients are obliged to provide certain basic information about their income, assets, and liabilities, but advisors need to go beyond that to assess their clients' risk profile and hence what type of investments would be suitable for them. If the client is reticent about elaborating on their basic information, it may be because the advisor has not established credibility with the client.[3] Advisors cannot expect clients to just open up in the first meeting. They must earn the trust of the client before the client will offer them their personal information.

So how do you earn that trust? By listening more, talking less, and letting the client set the agenda until they are comfortable with you. Only then can you ask meaningful questions and get meaningful answers. The key is to not rush them but instead listen to what they say, probe, and ultimately tell them what you can do to resolve their problems or concerns. If they have other advisors who they trust, whether they are accountants, lawyers, or other professionals, you might explore with the client why they find these advisors useful, credible, and trustworthy.

My advisor is credible and I trust her to take care of me and to give me advice that is in my best interest. How did my

---

2   This is an important aspect that distinguishes human advisors from the services offered by a robo-advisor.

3   For more on this, see Tim Hurson and Tim Dunne, *Never Be Closing: How to Sell Better Without Screwing Your Clients, Your Colleagues, or Yourself* (Penguin Publishing Group, 2014).

advisor earn my trust? She worked for a reputable dealer, she had been recommended by someone who I trusted, and she seemed to be a good listener. When we set up the account, she suggested that I pay a commission for trades because I don't do a lot of trading and it would be less expensive than paying an annual fee. I appreciated her advice but insisted that a fee would be better because I intended to call her about a number of financial issues. She said she would be pleased to give me that advice even if I paid her on a commission basis, but I still refused because I needed to feel that she was being paid for all services rendered.

How did she earn my trust sufficiently to obtain the information about my assets early in the relationship? I don't have many assets and I am generally quite an open person. However, I came to really trust my advisor when she suggested I do things that were not in her interest but in mine, like when my mortgage matured and she suggested I stay with my existing lender. Here's another example: She knows how much I hate debt. So, after I maxed out my RRSP contribution, we shoved as much money as possible against my mortgage, which she helped me negotiate as an open mortgage. Our goal was to pay it off entirely by the end of that year. We accomplished my goal, together.

She has become my partner in respect of all financial issues. She knows when I make more money. She knows when I get tax refunds and other inflows. She advises me to deposit the money into my account so that "we" can achieve the goals of "our" plan that we established with the help of a financial planner. She has a long-term approach to our relationship, from which she expects to ultimately benefit. In the meantime, she helps me solve financial problems, sometimes in ways that are of no immediate benefit to her.

She is building her reputation one client at a time, and she knows that her clients appreciate her service, and come to trust her. No doubt, this will serve to grow her business.

D. Clients just won't take responsibility for their investments—so how can an advisor succeed?

The problem is that many clients are not engaged in the relationship with their advisors. They think the advisor's role is just to take their money and, hopefully, make them money. They judge their advisors exclusively based on the returns on their investments. What these clients don't realize is that there are other goals their advisor could help them with, if only the advisor had enough information. Advisors cannot assess and advise without knowing their client's personal situations well beyond what is written down on the KYC form. (I hope to address this problem and help you convince your clients of the importance of being open by making available for download online the client guide that appears in the back of this book.)

Here is an example of a client and advisor who are not communicating properly. Sessi is a woman in her 50s who has been divorced for more than 10 years. Her RRSP account of $750,000 has been managed satisfactorily and returns have been sufficient. Sessi meets with her advisor each year, who also calls her when there are trades that must be done. Otherwise, she doesn't hear from him. What is missing? Client and advisor engagement. The advisor doesn't know that Sessi worries about money and whether she will have enough for her retirement. The advisor has not explored this with her, and she has not raised it.

Sessi learns from her friend about how the friend's advisor helps her resolve issues that cause her to worry about money.

Sessi signs papers to transfer her investments to her friend's advisor even though her returns were satisfactory with her existing advisor. Sessi's needs were not identified and as a result they were not met. This is the risk to advisors who fail to engage their clients.

In Sessi's case, she wanted more but she didn't know what "more" was and didn't articulate it to her advisor. Her advisor did not ask the right questions or attempt to engage Sessi in a meaningful way. The advisor needs to ask himself whether this was Sessi's refusal to share or his failure to engage her by asking the right questions.

i. Navel gazing

Could you have asked more questions and better engaged Sessi? Take this quiz to help you self-assess:

1. Do you hand your clients a questionnaire concerning their risk profile and accept their answers at face value? Or do you engage in discussions with them, asking probing questions to dig into why they answered as they did?

2. Do you ask clients the questions right from the KYC/NAAF (new account application form)? Or do you engage in open discussions concerning each question?[4]

3. When you ask your clients about their income, do you accept the number they present at face value? Or do you ask about prior years' income, expectations for the future, and

---

4   For an expansive discussion on the KYC process and what you need to do to fulfill your obligations, see *Advisor at Risk*, Chapter 3.

prospects for their industry or any future industries they are considering?[5]

4. When you ask clients about their financial knowledge, do you ask whether it is nil, low, medium, or high? Or do you ask about their education, formal and informal, to find out how they came to learn about money, savings, etc.?[6]

5. When you get to know your clients, do you avoid asking personal questions? Or do you inquire about any personal experiences that may have shaped their attitude toward money, savings, and other financial issues?

6. Do you ask your clients to describe their experiences, if any, of having made or lost money, whether it be from investments, gambling, real estate, etc.?

If you do not probe into these questions, the reason your client is not engaged in the process may be because you are not engaging them. This could be for many reasons:

- You don't feel comfortable asking personal questions.
- You don't think clients will be comfortable if you ask them personal questions.
- You are not interested in asking these questions.
- You are usually in a rush.

---

5   For a list of what to ask clients about their income, see *Advisor at Risk*, Chapter 3, page 53.

6   For more on client sophistication, see *Advisor at Risk*, Chapter 6, pages 87–89.

- You think your clients will be offended and won't open an account with you.
- It is not your style.

Clients take the lead from you. If you do not ask, they will not offer. If this is the limitation you have with your clients, you may want to reconsider your approach, both because it is what regulators and judges expect and because, without such engagement, you may find you are easily replaced by other advisors or even an online system such as a robo-advisor.

ii. *You can lead a horse to water, but . . .*

Few clients understand the degree to which they are responsible for their investments. Ideally, clients would meet with their advisors regularly to share their concerns and challenges, as well as their hopes and dreams. From this dialogue, the advisor and client develop—and carry out—an investment plan together. All the while, the advisor carefully manages the client's expectations. This is what I refer to as an "engaged" client, one who understands that it is their money and they must play a role in developing and carrying out the plan to meet their goals. But are all clients like that? Absolutely not.

Advisors need to explain clearly to clients their respective roles in this engagement. Clients must come to see they will be better served if they communicate their goals to their advisors, meet with them regularly, and work with them as partners.

You can lead a horse to water, but you cannot make it drink, the saying goes. There will always be those clients who insist that investing their money is the advisors' responsibility, not their own. I advise you to figure out early on who these clients are, and decide whether you want to work with them. If you take these clients on, it may increase your risk substantially. You may want to reconsider.

iii. *Judges will hold you to the same standard as other professionals*

Just how desperate are you to accept a client who refuses to impart the information you need to do your job? After all, you are a professional and are held to the same standard as professionals in other industries, such as lawyers and doctors.[7] Do you think professionals in other industries would accept a client who refuses to share information or who misleads them?

Let's look at an example of a doctor and patient:

PATIENT: I have a rash, see it?

DOCTOR: Is it itchy?

PATIENT: I am not telling, that is private.

DOCTOR: How long has it been there?

PATIENT: I am not telling, that is private and none of your business.

WHAT DO YOU think the doctor would say to such a client? This is what I think would happen next:

DOCTOR: I cannot treat you if you will not be transparent with me. Come back when you are prepared to give me the answers to these questions so that I can do my job.

TRANSPARENCY IS KEY to any client receiving useful advice from a professional.

---

7   *Rhoads v. Prudential-Bache Securities Canada Ltd.* (1992), 63 BCLR (2d) 256 (BCCA) at 262.

iv. *The deceptive client*

While you cannot read minds, professionals need to confront clients who they feel are giving them only part of the facts. I have had this happen to me. In this case, the advisor was the client who was not being transparent with me, and I was his (legal) advisor.

I met with an advisor who was being pursued by the regulator for signing (forging) his client's signature on forms. The advisor was being investigated and was asked by his dealer whether there were other occasions in which he signed for clients. The advisor told the dealer that it had only happened once, and that time was because the client had been sick and unable to sign. The advisor retained me because he was unsure how to deal with his dealer. He was worried because he knew the dealer was obliged to report this to the regulator. I asked the advisor whether he signed for clients other than the one in question. He told me he had not. I ask him if he was certain about this, and he said he was. I, of course, believed him.

As it turned out, his answer was untrue. The dealer did a further audit and found out that there were more forgeries. If the advisor had been honest with me and told me that there had been others, I would have told him to do an audit of his files to identify these other infractions. That way, he would be able to correct his answer to compliance immediately—before compliance identified other forgeries and the dealer fired him for lying. Remember, committing an infraction is one thing, but lying about it is actually a second infraction. Further, lying to your own advisor (lawyer) doesn't help you—it hurts you. This fact is exactly the same when it comes to your clients. You need to consider whether or not you can help a client who is not being transparent with you.

v. *Would you turn these clients away?*

It is hard to turn clients away, but if they are unengaged or holding back facts needed to service their account, working with them exposes you to unnecessary risk. Think about Dank and his hapless advisor from Chapter 1. Dank deceived his advisor by pretending to be a high roller when in truth he was chasing high returns—and high risk—to help pay for a lifestyle he could not afford. To avoid the risks such clients can expose you to, you need to:

- identify when a client is not being transparent with you;
- determine if you need to change how you approach the client to engage them;
- if you still are unable to engage them in a manner that permits you to do your job, consider the risks to which you expose yourself;
- based on your personal risk tolerance (as discussed in Chapter 3), determine if you can take the risk;
- if your risk tolerance is such that you are not prepared to take the risk, tell the client you cannot continue to work with them; or
- if you can take the risk, keep working with the client, trying to engage them to get the entire story.

E. KYC updates

Not being diligent with Know Your Client updates creates both missed opportunities and exposure.

i. *Updates: why?*

There is an industry epidemic that leads to lost opportunities when it comes to KYC form updates. While advisors are required to get KYC form updates from clients, they often complain that the document is a waste of everyone's time and is a meaningless regulatory requirement. While I am the first to criticize the regulators for adding another form to the mix to fix every problem, there is a reason for updates to KYC forms. How can advisors know that a client's circumstances have changed if they do not have meaningful conversations for the purpose of updating the KYC form?

Yet many advisors carry out this update requirement in the following way: They direct their administrative assistant to fill in the update form with the old KYC information and send it to the client for signature. Sometimes there is a telephone call to alert clients in advance that the update is being mailed and they need to sign it and return it. The call from the administrative assistant (or sometimes the advisor) goes something like this:

ADMIN/ADVISOR: Hello, Mr. Smith, I need you to sign a form that serves to update your information. Have there been any changes in your financial situation?

MR. SMITH: No.

ADMIN/ADVISOR: Okay, you will receive a form in the mail. Kindly sign it and send it back in the enclosed self-addressed and stamped envelope. Thank you.

If, when the advisor calls Mr. Smith, there is no answer, then the advisor leaves a message alerting Mr. Smith that he will receive a form in the mail and he is to sign and send it back or call if there are any changes that need to be made. Alternatively, there could be a cover letter sent with the form, explaining all of this. Does the advisor get a call back? Not likely. Does the advisor even get the signed form returned to him? Not likely.

Updating the form in this manner leads to advisors missing important changes to a client's circumstances. This defeats the purpose of the update requirement. It's also important to consider that following this process creates a missed opportunity to communicate with the client in a meaningful way and thereby deepen your relationship. Furthermore, such half-hearted communication increases your regulatory and litigation risk, as regulators and dealers may realize, through an audit or client complaint, that you are not meeting your obligations in a meaningful way.

When I discuss this problem with advisors, they suggest that their clients don't want to spend the time with them and, more often than not, their calls to clients about updates are not returned. This is a problem for advisors, especially when the deadline for updated forms is looming. As a result, compliance sends a barrage of email reminders that serve to badger the advisor.[8]

But when I'm told this: I wonder. Is the client not responding because the exercise of signing the form is of no value to them? Or is the client just too busy to meet or respond to their advisor? Either way, this exercise has become not just a lost opportunity but also a risk to the advisor and their clients, whose account may contain unsuitable investments that do not reflect changed circumstances.

ii. How can advisors resolve this gap?
You can bridge the gap between you and your clients by

---

8   Advisors have been known to sign for clients in these circumstances. But the regulators have been clamping down heavily in this area, penalizing many advisors in public hearings—mostly settlement hearings.

making the exercise of updating a KYC form meaningful to them. How? Follow these steps:

1. Show how it benefits them. You need to get the form signed. Your client needs to ensure you know about any changes in their situation, and that you will adjust their investments accordingly. A meaningless telephone call or letter puts the advisor's needs first and doesn't factor in the client's needs. A voicemail or letter telling them that you have an obligation to fill is not a compelling reason for them to call back. The client does not think they can benefit from this exercise, and, as a result, you cannot benefit either. To ensure that the exercise is meaningful to the client, explain and define the terms and forms and their importance to the client.

2. Take interest. As I have said before, advisors need to have a genuine interest in any changes that might affect their clients, and what those changes might mean when it comes to properly managing client portfolios or selling them the right insurance product. This genuine interest will permeate through every communication with clients, making it more compelling for them to meet or talk with you.

3. Make the effort, or pass it on. If you have too many small accounts, or accounts that you believe do not merit the time necessary to have a meaningful meeting, think again. Either keep them and service them in a compliant and meaningful way, or get them to transfer to another advisor or robo/discount account to reduce your risk of being accused of failing to fulfill your regulatory and legal obligations.

4. Don't rush. Clients may not freely share private information with their advisor. It might take some probing, but that is what makes the relationship more meaningful and engaging for clients. That is the goal!

5. Do it yourself. Client updates cannot be delegated to other advisors or to your assistants, even if the account is small. You, as the advisor, have an obligation to know your client at every stage of the relationship. This is an important task that you are required to do yourself.

Summary

Clear and consistent communication between advisors and clients leads to success. While growing your business, it is important to protect your existing clients by understanding them and taking a genuine interest in them. You can achieve this by listening carefully to what clients say, taking the time to understand their needs, solving problems for them, putting their needs first (even if there is no immediate pay-off), and keeping up with changes in their lives.

Advisors Take Action

✓ Build a strong business foundation by adopting processes to exceed your clients' expectations.

✓ Understand your clients. Learn your clients' backstories and remember those stories when making recommendations.

✓ Earn your clients' trust by listening more and talking less. Let each client set the agenda until they are comfortable with you.

✓ Ask meaningful personal questions to engage your clients.

✓ Explain clearly to your clients that they will be better served if they communicate their goals to you, meet with you regularly, and work with you as their partner.

✓ Make the KYC update exercise meaningful to your clients by showing a genuine interest in any changes that might affect them. Explain and define the terms and forms and their importance to the client. Do not delegate this task.

✓ Remember, if you do a great job for your existing clients, they will want you to succeed.

5

Advisor and Client—
Know Your Product

GONE ARE THE days when an advisor could make decisions to buy or sell and not explain the reasoning behind the strategy and the choice of product to the client. The old regime of knowing your product required merely a superficial understanding. You can no longer get by with this approach. This chapter will focus on the higher standard that advisors need to meet to ensure clients have a clear understanding of their investments, whether those be securities or insurance products.[1] Educating yourself about each product is an important ingredient to surviving in this industry. Further, being able to explain those products to clients, and prove they understand them, is key.

---

1   See *Advisor at Risk*, Chapter 5, for the basics of this topic.

If advisors are unable to prove that this standard is met, they open a big communication gap, and they risk paying a price for it. Here, I will home in on the risks that I have observed while representing advisors at regulatory proceedings and in litigation.

To change your current practice in respect of Know Your Product (KYP), or any other aspect of your business, the first step is to change your thinking and attitude. To do that, it is important to understand the risks of not doing so. As you read this chapter, keep these two aspects in mind:

1. Clients complain and sue when they are surprised about anything relating to their portfolio, and particularly so when it concerns risks associated with any aspect of the product that they say they were not told about in advance. The most common surprise is risk associated with products or strategies that, in retrospect, they argue were unsuitable.

2. Without a solid paper trail proving that the advisor explained the characteristics and risks associated with a product, and that the client understood these risks, the advisor may not succeed against the client.

Here is an example of an advisor I defended. Let's call him Mikka. Mikka didn't fulfill his KYP and suitability obligations. As a result, he paid a big price. Not only did he end up having to pay a financial penalty, he also suffered damage to his reputation that came from the matter being posted on the regulator's website for existing and potential clients to see.

Four of Mikka's clients alleged that he had purchased the same unsuitable investments for their accounts. These clients, not knowledgeable or sophisticated when it came to investing, knew each other, so when one complained about the losses arising from these investments, the others followed. To counter the allegations, Mikka supplied the regulator with emails and notes from his files that confirmed telephone calls and regular annual meetings with these clients. However, none of the emails or notes confirmed that Mikka had explained the product—specifically, the product risks—to these clients.

Mikka was challenged by the regulator on this issue. The regulator asked Mikka for evidence of what he knew about the products at the time of the transactions, and what he explained to each of the four complaining clients—along with what they understood. The advisor fell short in his response, because he didn't seem to understand the complexity of the products, or wasn't able to explain them to the regulator. His notes from client meetings did not include anything that reflected discussions about the product qualities or risks.

Furthermore, when challenged by the regulator, Mikka could not prove that this product choice was consistent with the clients' needs or that he had explained the strategies and the products to the clients.

What could Mikka have done differently?

I. Don't Turn Product Risks into Advisor Risks!

The first step for all advisors is to study the product, and its potential risks, and maintain a paper trail of what was reviewed.[2] Superficial knowledge based only on a review of the marketing materials is insufficient.

---

2 When I say 'paper trail', this could be a 'soft' trail in your computer, backed up regularly, to ensure these materials are available years after the investment is made.

A. Know the product risks

For each product,[3] study and digest the different types of risks and how they impact the particular product. These risks include but are not limited to: business cycles (the boom and bust nature of cyclical businesses such as real estate and commodities), changes in the economy (inflation and interest rates), market fluctuations, currency and industry shifts, politics (both local and international), supply and demand, liquidity risk, and risks mentioned or caused by attention in the media (TV, social media, comments on the internet, blogs).

If the product is subject to any particular risks, how is the balance of the portfolio diversified to ensure other products are chosen to counterbalance the risks of a particular product?[4] It is not just about examining any one product in a vacuum; it is about building the entire portfolio. This is so that you can later explain to regulators and judges that you designed the portfolio to fit together and be properly diversified.

I have reviewed many client accounts that were not balanced in this manner. Even an account that contains a single, highly diversified product (such as a balanced fund) could be examined for failing to be sufficiently diversified because there is only one management team making decisions.[5] Diversification among managers can be as important as diversification in product choice.

---

3   I prepared a "cheat sheet" to help advisors understand these products, which can be printed off as a separate document at www.babinbessnerspry.com/kyp.pdf.

4   Of course, there are those high-risk investments that sophisticated and experienced clients may choose to overload on and in which the client can afford to lose the money. These accounts are not expected to be balanced. However, ensure that you can indeed prove that the client was sophisticated and that this was the purpose of the account.

5   A portfolio that might seem to be heavily weighted in one investment may not be when considering the client's assets outside the dealer.

For every product you recommend, you need to fully appreciate the risks and how they could impact the product's performance. So, how can you make sure you are up-to-date and informed? Read on.

B. Study and keep a list

A product manufacturer's marketing presentations and materials highlight and summarize the product's benefits. In the past, the advisor could get away with simply reviewing these materials to fulfill all obligation to know the product. That has all changed. So do your research.

The first step is to read everything available about the product,[6] including the prospectus, analyst reports, company press releases, articles in the media, and any other materials available.

Consider this, in case you are not convinced that you need to read the prospectus: advisors are regularly hauled in by various regulators and specifically asked, "Did you read the prospectus or the offering memorandum associated with the product before you sold it?" Answering honestly,[7] many admit they did not. That is evidence regulators can use against advisors for failing to know their products at the time of sale.

Read carefully and make notes, electronically or otherwise. Keep a list of what you read and what you learned from what you read. The more complex the product, the more you need to study. I know this sounds like a lot of work, but before any

---

6   For more on this, see my article "Don't shoot the messenger: Understanding the products you sell requires a lot more than just reading the marketing material," July 14, 2014, *Investment Executive*, Inside Track; see also *Advisor at Risk*, Chapter 5, page 82.

7   While it can be tempting to answer yes when asked if you have reviewed materials that you have not, it is worse to lie about it, as this lie is another infraction, one leading to an additional penalty, which may be much worse.

product lands in one of your client's accounts, you need to have a PhD in that product and need to be able to prove it.

C. What should you read?

Here is a basic list of things to read and issues to consider in your study of investment products. This is just a beginning, so don't feel restricted by this list:

- The prospectus or Offering Memoranda (OM). I can assure you that the regulator will ask you whether you read the prospectus/OM in the interview, and I don't want you to be caught by surprise. Some of these sections in the prospectus/OM are not about the actual product—and you could skim those. However, the portions that drill down on the elements of the product, the risks, who should invest, and how the product might be affected by market fluctuations are key elements that must be read carefully.

- Company releases posted on SEDAR.

- Analyst reports.

- Internet postings.

- Your securities dealer file that was reviewed before the product was placed on the dealer's shelf. This might be historic, but it should also be updated regularly.

- Any alerts that you can subscribe to that might provide real-time information as the product changes.

- For insurance products, the information folder and other product documentation from the insurance carrier.[8]

D. Questions to ask yourself about the product

Again, this list is not comprehensive, but these questions are a good place to begin:

- Is the product similar to one you have in-depth knowledge of? How is it different?

- Is the product unique? What makes it unique?

- Is the complexity and risk of the product high, low, or medium? Why?

- Are there embedded costs with the product? These need to be understood.

- Is the product illiquid? What makes it illiquid?

- In what circumstances can clients redeem the product? Is there a penalty attached to redemptions at any time? When and how do they redeem?

- Does the product have embedded leverage? Leverage renders a product more risky, so you need to understand when it is used, how much (i.e., the ratio), how this borrowing increases risk and the impact paying interest will have on returns.

---

8   See the Canadian Life and Health Insurance Association (CLHIA) Guidelines.

- Are the 'anticipated returns' suggested by the issuer realistic? What were the previous returns compared to the projections? Do previous returns cover periods from one, three, and five years, or is it a relatively new product? Do you think the past and anticipated returns are accurately recorded, and if not, why not? Don't just accept this at face value.

- Is a portion, or the entire amount, of returns in the form of a return of the client's own capital? If so, what is the benefit to the client?

- What are the tax implications of the product, if any? Are there tax benefits, and if so, are they overstated? Is there a caution that any tax benefit might become inapplicable if new legislation is passed?

- What is it about this product that is particularly attractive, i.e., why was this product chosen over other similar products. You should have a good reason for choosing this product over others.[9]

- Are you properly treating cash as a considered product? Cash generates no returns[10] but there might be a reason

---

9   This issue is presently in flux at the time of writing, as regulators are considering reforms to the KYP obligations: CSA Consultation Paper 33-404, "Proposals to enhance the obligations of advisers, dealers, and representatives towards their clients," April 28, 2016, available at www.osc.gov.on.ca/documents/en/Securities-Category3/csa_20160428_33-404_proposals-enhance-obligations-advisers-dealers-representatives.pdf.

10   There are possibly positive or negative implications due to strengthening/weakening of the dollar and deflation/inflation.

for keeping cash in an account, such as a client's fears of a correction or simply their direct instructions. However, if the client pays a fee based on the assets in the account, rather than a commission for each transaction, the advisor or portfolio manager might be exposed, as a fee is being charged on the cash portion of the portfolio that is sitting idle and not earning any dividends or returns.[11]

- Do you understand your dealer's operating model? This includes what is promoted, and what is not. Much of this is clear from the dealer's policy and procedures manual and the message expressed, from time to time, from the top (compliance or senior management). For example, if a product is purchased using leverage or margin (borrowing to invest), is this part of the dealer culture or not?

II. Communication: Explaining to the Client

Regulators want to determine if the advisor understood the product before they turn to finding out whether the client understood the product. The theory is that if an advisor didn't understand a product, or the model and approach applied to client accounts, that advisor couldn't determine whether it was suitable for the client and, further, would have been unable to explain it to the client. Regulators suggest that if the client did not understand the product, then that is enough to conclude that the product was unsuitable for the client.

---

11 One of the few portfolio manager reported decisions, and a case worth reading, is 2878852 *Canada Inc. v. Jones Heward Investment Counsel Inc.* (2004), Carswell Ont. 3393, affirmed 2007, ONCA 14.

I know that doesn't really follow logically because a product may be complicated but the risk of the product may be appropriate for the client. Most people would conclude that if the risk of the product matches the client's risk profile, the product should be suitable. This is not the perception of the regulators or judges. They are of the view that for the client to buy a product, they must understand what it is and how it works.

Here is another aspect of being able to prove that you understood the product: If you, the advisor, are intelligent, educated, and experienced but still do not understand the product, then how can a client who is not as financially knowledgeable possibly understand it?

Another potential red flag: If, again, an intelligent, educated, and experienced advisor is unable to understand the product sufficiently to explain it to the client, then perhaps the product issuer is making it that complicated because they don't want the advisor or the client to understand it. Issuers who sell products that are not clear may be trying to hide something. If there is something to hide and the advisor did not dig sufficiently into the product to identify the problems, and the issuer is then put up in front of the regulator, the advisor could be dragged into it as well.

So how can all of these challenges be summarized, and how can an advisor overcome each of them?

Challenge 1: How do you ensure you can explain it at the client's level of understanding?

i. *Know and prove each client's ability to understand*
The first step is to have a clear understanding of the client's financial experience and sophistication level, to ensure that

you adjust your explanations accordingly. You have to get into their head to learn what they know and what they don't know, what they do and do not understand. Only when you do this can you properly explain to clients what they need to understand before they invest. You will need to take notes and keep other evidence to prove that you have done so, especially if the client's KYC form shows little or no investment experience.[12]

ii. Practice explaining each product and product type at a basic level

If you are intending to sell certain products, you will need to develop a way to explain each of the products clearly and fully. Even those clients who sign a KYC indicating they are higher than "nil" on the sophistication chart tend to later assert, when they are making a complaint, that they had little or no experience or knowledge and were not sophisticated investors. So knowing how to explain the product at a more basic level, and being able to prove it, will reduce your risk.

I have defended many matters in which extremely sophisticated and experienced clients complaining of losses assert that they were novice investors who didn't understand anything, and that their advisors provided no explanations. They do this regardless of what is indicated on the know-your-client forms that they signed.

Remember, it is easier to explain something at a higher level than at a more basic level. Sometimes being unable to explain a product at a basic level is a sign that you don't fully understand the product. Other times, you do fully understand

---

12   For more on this, see *Advisor at Risk*, Chapter 6, in which the element of 'sophistica-tion' is explored deeply.

it, but can get "lost in the weeds" when trying to explain it to a client. I suggest that you practice each explanation on someone you know who has only a very basic understanding of financial matters, like a friend or family member. Encourage them to ask questions, and to stop you when they don't understand. Use simple language, not terms of the trade (e.g., 'standard deviation') or acronyms.[13] This will help you recognize whether your clients fully understand what you are endeavoring to explain to them.

iii. Use the internet

The web is a great resource for simple definitions of different types of products. You can source these basic definitions to help unsophisticated clients understand the difference between mutual funds, stocks, bonds, exchange-traded funds, etc. You may also find materials to help you explain more complicated concepts to more sophisticated clients, like puts, calls, or embedded leverage. There may be helpful tools on regulators and SRO websites as well.

Keep records of where you source your definitions from and what you explain to clients. That way, if you are called on the regulator/SRO carpet or hauled into court to answer questions concerning what you learned and what definitions you used, you will be prepared and able to prove that your explanations were at the same level and consistent with the messages, concerns, and values expressed in these websites.

---

13 See *Advisor at Risk*, Chapter 2, for more on speaking in a manner that clients can understand.

Challenge 2: How do you prove that the client understood?

i. *Cautionary note #1: Sophisticated clients*

Before I get started with suggestions to help you prove that your clients understood what you were telling them, I want to caution you not to skip this section, thinking that your clients are mostly sophisticated so there is no need to prove that they understood a particular product or strategy. You need objective evidence in each client's file to prove to a judge or regulator that the client had the background and ability to understand. However, even with that, sophisticated clients may claim to be unsophisticated. When that happens, you are left having to prove that they understood what was explained to them about the product or strategy.

ii. *Cautionary note # 2: Managed products*

There is a shift by advisors to not do their own product selection but instead recommend their dealer's managed product to clients. In this case, your primary responsibility then becomes managing the relationship, rather than the investments. So, what are your responsibilities in these circumstances?

Your responsibilities are the same. You need to ensure the managed products you choose are consistent with your client's risk profile. You also need to ensure your client understands the managed product, what it consists of, and what the strategy is. As the managed product investments change, you need to be on top of those changes and explain them to your clients during regular meetings. Passive investments do not mean you can be passive about your duty. Your duties remain the same.

iii. Cautionary note #3: Portfolio managers

Portfolio managers (PMs) have discretion over their clients' accounts and can buy and sell without instructions as long as the trades are consistent with the Investment Policy Statement and the KYC form. As a result, PMs may be inclined to disregard this chapter because their obligation to obtain permission to trade is not required. However, you would be wrong to think it is safe to keep your clients in the dark about product and strategy choices. Remember, clients tend to sue when they are surprised. Clients of portfolio managers may be more apt to be surprised because the contact required is far less than what is required of a mutual fund salesperson or investment advisor. I encourage any portfolio managers reading this to keep your clients apprised of investment choices and strategies by meeting with them regularly. Your clients tend to be high net worth, and so have the resources to sue—and they do! When portfolio managers are sued, their ability to shift responsibility to the client is limited due to the fiduciary duty that a portfolio manager has to clients.[14]

iv. The importance of in-person meetings

The most effective communication occurs during in-person meetings. When you're sitting in front of a client, you can watch their facial expressions and body language to help determine whether they understand what you are saying. You want the client to feel comfortable enough to ask questions. In-person meetings, assuming they are not rushed, might be the best way to get clients to express concerns and become more engaged in the investing process.

---

14 While there is a push by regulators to change the standard required by all advisors to that of fiduciary, this has not occurred at the time of writing.

v. Don't rush

Make sure that both you and your client have set aside enough time to cover everything you need to. If the client has to make a decision about an investment by a certain deadline, try to find an interim alternative to ensure the client is not squeezed into making a snap decision.

vi. Client engagement is key

Proving that your client understood what you were saying requires that you ensure they are sufficiently engaged in the process. This can be particularly difficult when you are meeting with more than one person, for example, a client and their spouse. Sometimes one spouse is more engaged in the process than the other, so you naturally direct your attention to the one who is more engaged. This can also happen when an elderly client brings a trusted friend or family member to the meeting. If you direct your conversation to the friend or family member, the elderly client might disengage and therefore not understand or remember what was explained. Be mindful of this pitfall.

vii. Use an agenda to spell out what you intend to explain

It is difficult to take notes when you are speaking, but you can prepare an agenda of the points you are going to explain. Tick off each item as you discuss it. By doing this, you will have a paper trail without having to write and speak at the same time. If your agenda sets out the product features, including the pros and cons, you can later prove what you told the client about the product. Simply date the agenda at the top and tick off each item as you go over it. If you want the client to sign that you discussed each of the agenda items, that would be golden, but it is not necessary. Remember, clients tend to deny receiving explanations. But if you have the date, time, and other details of each telephone call and meeting, the client will not likely be believed. This is particularly true if you follow this method each time you meet with the client and have several of these agendas in the file. Electronic or scanned copies should be fine, although courts prefer originals, if possible.

viii. Encourage and accurately document client questions

While a detailed agenda goes a long way to support the fact that you explained the risks, it will not necessarily support your position that the client understood. This is especially so because most clients deny understanding these explanations later when they sue, claiming the investment or strategy was unsuitable. However, if the client asks a question, this can prove that 1) the client was engaged in the process, and 2) the client understood sufficiently to ask a question (or two, or more). Make a habit of writing down client questions in quotes. You can refer to them later if you are interrogated about whether the client understood. This would be powerful evidence.

ix. Most complaining clients allege they were unsophisticated

Remember that while many clients are sophisticated, later when they launch a complaint, they will say they are not. If the judge or regulator believes that the client is unsophisticated, the advisor will have to prove that their explanation was simple enough. Even if the client did not come across as unsophisticated throughout the relationship, it is up to you to determine how simply you want to explain the product/strategy to each client.

x. Ask clients questions to reflect their understanding

You can ask clients questions that evoke comments reflecting their understanding of what you discussed. For example, you can ask what they think of the two products you discussed and which they prefer. You can ask what the most important features were of the products you discussed. Don't let them get off with a one-word answer. Ask them why they prefer one over the other. Make notes of what they say. If they say they like product X because of the favorable tax consequences, make detailed notes of these explanations, because they show the client understood. If they say they don't know, or have no preference, that may be a sign they do not understand and that you may have to explain further.

xi. The importance of two-way written communication

It is not enough to send written materials to clients and ask them to read the information. Advisors have told me on several occasions that they "communicate" with clients every month. I learn, however, these are one-way communications through newsletters or mass emails. Newsletters are great for marketing, but they are not a replacement for two-way communication, in which products and strategies are specifically explained. When regulators or judges review the paper trail, they are looking for notes, emails, or letters clarifying, explaining, or confirming conversations. If there is a two-way exchange between a client and an advisor that confirms discussions, this will show that the client understood and was engaged in the process. Two-way communication can be contained in emails, too. I see cases in which clients assert they didn't understand the investments, yet the advisor has emails in which the client weighs in on decisions about whether to buy, sell, or hold and why. That is a gold mine for me as defense counsel!

xii. Send confirming emails

While you cannot take orders by email, you can certainly confirm explanations provided by email. You can also set out in an email the questions asked and answered. I do this all the time when clients ask me about something important and I want to make sure they understood our discussion and can reflect upon it after our meeting. While I might have answered verbally, I later set it out in writing. This not only helps them understand, it helps them to consider any other issues or questions arising from my explanation. If my client is ever concerned about how a decision was made on their file, the paper trail of emails will permit me to remind them that we had a discussion. It will also serve to remind me of this exchange. If the client asks me how the decision was made and there isn't any paper trail, I would struggle to remember (and it is very unlikely that I could remember years after, when this would likely be raised). I would be at a loss and exposed if my client suggested they were not properly consulted.

xiii. Refer clients to web portals for investor education

While investor education cannot replace your explanations, it can help advisors get their clients up to speed about investments or other financial matters. Feel free to refer relevant materials from the investor education sections on the websites of the provincial securities commissions, MFDA, and IIROC. An unsophisticated client is more likely to understand the information on these sites than some other types of investor materials, like a prospectus, and they might even receive more detailed information than what is in the fund facts. While these must be sent to clients by law, even sophisticated clients are unlikely to read them, even if they should. Investor education sites are geared specifically to clients and may be more relevant to them.

Seniors are definitely the riskiest segment of the population for advisors because regulators and judges believe them to be vulnerable. While seniors may have more time to read materials, if they have cognitive issues, this may not be an option. However, if they have the ability to understand what they read, send them hard copies or, if they are computer literate, links to such investor education sites. In future communication, try to use the same jargon that the sites use, so that there is consistency.

III. Unsolicited Trades: What Is Your KYP Duty If a Client Wants to Choose the Product?

I am frequently asked about the advisor's duty when the client wants to pick the product or strategy. "For unsolicited trades, must the advisor know the product in order to buy it for the client?" My answer is a resounding "Yes." Advisors who buy a security for a client need to know the product, regardless of who initiated the trade. Let me present three different scenarios that will demystify the advisor's obligations regarding investments that clients have initiated.

Scenario 1

Mr. U tells you that he wants to buy XYZ, a security you are following and that you understand to be well matched for Mr. U's goals and risk profile. Of course, you can buy this security as long as it is suitable and fits Mr. U's portfolio. Still, you need to explain any risks or concerns about XYZ, and not assume Mr. U is aware of them just because he was the one to suggest the trade.

Despite the fact the trade is marked 'unsolicited'—and indicated as such in the client management system and on client statements—it is important to continue to follow the product to ascertain if and when it should be sold.

Scenario 2

Mr. U tells you he wants ABC in his account as he believes it to be a 'sure winner', but you do not know about or follow ABC. The correct response here is to tell Mr. U to buy this in a self-directed discount brokerage account because it does not make sense to pay you a commission for a product you know nothing about. If Mr. U insists on buying ABC in his full-service account—and you have no intention of following this product—you should check with compliance. The terms and conditions of the account likely permit you to refuse the trade, which is what you should do.

If you do agree to buy ABC for the client, then you will need to learn about the product, to ensure not only that it is suitable for Mr. U but also that Mr. U understands any risks or concerns you might have about it or the issuer. Let us assume, for this scenario, that the investment is suitable, you can buy it, and you mark the trade 'unsolicited'. Now you must follow the product to ascertain when to sell. But what if you conclude that the product is unsuitable? That brings us to the next scenario.

Scenario 3

The facts here are the same as with scenario 2 (you don't follow the product), but you are pretty sure that ABC is unsuitable for Mr. U based on the little you know about it. The only compliant option here is for you to refuse the trade and suggest that if the client wants to buy the security, he should do so in a discount or self-directed account. The terms and conditions of the account likely permit the advisor to make this refusal.

If the client is adamant, insisting that he will miss an opportunity and sue for any profits he missed, then you might want to execute the trade and give him notice that he should immediately move his account, or to move this unsuitable investment out of the account. This needs to be confirmed in writing.

So what is the benefit of marking the trade 'unsolicited' if you are still obliged to follow the product? Although doing so has little regulatory benefit, it can help in litigation in the following ways: 1) it can be evidence of sophistication if the client has initiated trades, and 2) if the client sues for losses on an unsolicited trade, the damages are more likely to, at least partly, flow to the client.[15]

Summary

Now more than ever, judges and regulators require advisors to make absolutely sure their clients have a clear understanding of their investments. Advisors may be held accountable for any communication gap. Educating yourself thoroughly about each product is key to being able to explain each product to your clients and to prove they understood.

------

15   See for example, *Negligence Act,* RSO 1990 c.N-1 in Ontario; *Contributory Negligence Act,* RSA. 2000 c. C-27 in Alberta; *Negligence Act,* RSBC chapter 333 in British Columbia; *Contributory Negligence Act,* RS c.95 in Nova Scotia.

Advisors Take Action

✓ Study each product and the potential risks thoroughly by reading the prospectus, analyst reports, company press releases, articles in the media, and any other materials available. Maintain a detailed paper trail of what you reviewed.

✓ Make sure you have a clear understanding of your clients' financial experience and sophistication level to ensure that you adjust your explanations accordingly.

✓ Conduct in-person meetings to explain products to your clients. Use an agenda to keep track of what you explained. Check in on whether the client is engaged by encouraging them to ask questions, and ask the client questions that reflect their understanding. Document all client questions and confirm explanations provided by email.

✓ Remember, you have a duty to know and follow the product even if the client initiates the investment.

6

Client Risk

––––––––––

SUITABILITY[1] IS THE riskiest part of this industry, as it is at the heart of most client complaints to regulators and in litigation. It is also more complex than you might appreciate. At the heart of suitability is determining the client's appetite for risk. The client's risk profile is a multilayered concept that needs unpacking to enable advisors to apply it properly.

In this chapter, we will take a deep dive into the different elements of risk profiles so that you can appreciate how communication is a key ingredient to making an accurate determination of client risk. Communication here involves asking the right questions and exploring beyond clients' initial superficial answers to ensure risk profiles are assessed accurately and clients are invested suitably.

––––––––––

1   See also *Advisor at Risk*, Chapter 4.

I. Why Is Suitability the Basis for Most Client Complaints?

Why is suitability such a problem? Suitability requires the advisor to understand the client, understand the products, and match them appropriately. Therefore, suitability is a combination of four potential failures on the part of the advisor, listed below. The first two failures were discussed in the previous chapter. The second two I will look at here, in depth.

1. Applying faulty methods of choosing the product mix to match each client's risk profile and of ensuring clients are properly diversified.

2. Failing to explain the risk to clients in a manner that they can understand and for which they can take responsibility.

3. Failing to know clients sufficiently to determine their risk profile, both at the time of initial assessment and as time goes on, as a client's circumstances change.

4. Failing to understand the different components of developing a client risk profile, overweighting one component, or not sufficiently factoring in others.

At the heart of all four issues is a failure to properly communicate with clients. It is necessary to ask questions; to listen carefully, attempting to set aside your own biases; to probe; and to properly analyze what the client has said. These failures, coupled with the complexity of suitability, make it easier for clients to find sufficient fault to support lawsuits.

II. A Deep Dive into Suitability

There are many aspects an advisor needs to take into consideration when it comes to suitability.

A. KYC aspects that affect risk profile analysis

Because almost every aspect of the KYC form impacts the analysis of a client's risk profile, you have to get each element of the KYC right in order to accurately determine the totality of a client's risk profile.

Good listening skills are key to getting this right. It means that the client does most of the talking, and you do most of the listening, taking notes and asking open-ended questions.[2] Every time you speak to the client, you need to home in on what they say to determine if there is anything that might cause you to rethink their risk profile.

This KYC exercise is broken down into three categories: 1) demographic and factual, 2) knowledge and experience, and 3) risk assessment. From here, I will examine each, and then move into a discussion of risk profiling.

Category 1: Demographic and factual

a. What is in a name?

While there may be nothing in a name, there might also be something. Your client's name may evoke a story.

In a multicultural environment, a name might indicate the background of someone's husband, father, or mother. The client might be from a war-torn country or a descendant of

---

2   For a closer review of open-ended questions, see *Advisor at Risk*, pages 29-30.

holocaust survivors. Or they might belong to a wealthy and prominent family. This could lead to conversations and information being gathered about the client that might affect their decision-making when it comes to investing.

Be very careful not to make assumptions or rely on stereotypes. Just because you have heard that certain traits concerning finances are typical of people from certain backgrounds, assuming your client fits the bill could be dead wrong. You will want to discuss with the client the impact of coming from a war-torn country or being a holocaust survivor or from the third generation of a well-known family. There might be significant financial implications, not just for a possible inheritance but also for their emotional relationship with money. So give the client's name some thought. It might be an important gateway to discussing and understanding their fears or motivations.

b. Where your client lives, and the power of WHY

Why does your client live where they do? Do they own their home outright, or do they have a mortgage? Why did they choose that particular city or neighborhood? Do they live with someone else or alone? In asking these questions, you are delving into how your client finances their home, and whether someone else is helping to pay for it—likely without having to come right out and ask.

Even before you get into their net worth, asking "why" can help you determine how clients feel about debt. For example, asking why they live in a rental home when they earn a substantial income may lead to an explanation that they are uncomfortable having a mortgage and hate debt. In this case, asking "why" has given you insight into aspects of their risk profile, even before these are examined. A client may express a nervousness about the future. Or the client may think they are unable to afford to purchase even though, objectively, that is not the case.

On the other hand, if the client has taken a bigger mortgage than seems reasonable, asking "why" may give insight into their values. A conversation about "why" on issues that seem mundane can give you better insight than proposing an answer that may be wrong.

Asking about the amount of their mortgage, for example, will only give you information concerning their debt, unless you also ask the question "why." If the answer then gives you insight into an aversion to debt, this could give you an entrée to a further discussion of "why," which might lead to a full conversation about risk. For example, are they concerned about the risk of losing their home to the lending institution? Are they nervous about owing money? Do they dislike paying interest? Or do they feel unsure about setting down roots and prefer flexibility?

Knowing this will give you greater insight into a client's attitude toward money than you would get by simply asking only about their debt load. It is more natural and authentic to have a conversation. As well, it may prompt the client to reflect on how they feel about these things.

c. The effect of age

While age in a vacuum may not have direct implications, it is how age impacts time horizon that, in turn, impacts the client's risk profile. Academics suggest advisors might be putting too much emphasis on age to assess risk profiles, as studies have shown that age does not impact risk to any noticeable extent.[3] However, the regulators, in an effort to protect seniors as a segment of vulnerable clients, consider age an important factor and regularly question advisors with elderly clients in high-risk investments. The topic of seniors and suitability will be further explored in Chapter 9, particularly the paper trail required to satisfy regulators that high-risk investments might be suitable for elderly clients.

d. Marital status: the implications

Both present and past marital status might impact suitability, but inquiring about the client's current marital status will not give you this information. A more in-depth conversation about past, present, and future will give you more insight.

Present and past marital status may affect the client's financial position. Much of this will depend on whether they are supporting a partner and/or children, or whether both contribute to the expenses, evenly or unevenly. The question of "how" becomes important. Whether currently in a relationship, or as a result of a previous relationship, how family expenses get covered and by whom is critical information. Does your client or their partner have past partners from previous relationships to support, and how is that financed? Regular payments to support previous partners, or the sole financial burden of supporting others, may lead to clients having less flexibility to adapt to bad markets, especially if they rely on their investments for this support. All of this will affect the client's ability to save and invest money.

---

3   See the report "Current practices for risk profiling in Canada and review of global best practices," November 2015, by Shawn Brayman, Dr. Michael Finke, Dr. Paul Griffin and myself for the Investor Advisory Panel of the OSC, page 43. Available at www.osc .gov.on.ca/documents/en/Investors/iap_20151112_risk-profiling-report.pdf.

Another important aspect to explore is the attitude of the client's partner toward money and finances. While this is not directly on the KYC form, this information will give you further insight into your client's obligations and financial position. For example, if a present or former partner is a big spender who likes to live beyond their means, your client might be affected by the stress this could place on the family finances.

Of course, a divorce can have financial implications, too, particularly if your client must support two families. All of these considerations might have significant implications for the client's risk profile.

e. Vocation

Vocation may have implications beyond knowing what the client does for a living, if the right questions are asked. In your discussions with clients, explore past employment and future prospects, even though these are beyond what is required on the KYC form. Both are important in determining suitability.

Why are they important? If the client has a stable job that has reliably and amply provided for them throughout their life, this speaks to their ability to support themselves and contribute to their investment account and, therefore, weather investment loss. Whether the client's spouse or life partner is in a stable job might also affect the client in this manner.

On the other hand, as is more common these days, if your client has a career path that has been uneven and unpredictable, then there may be more changes in the future. The client might need to reinvent themselves, which can mean more education and costly downtime. These changes need to be examined in detail through ongoing conversations. Investments may need to be adjusted for risk level and/or liquidity.

f. Income from all sources

Many advisors ask one simple question from the KYC form: "What is your annual income?" Perhaps the client replies, "$100,000," then this advisor simply fills in that information on the form. That's it! In doing so, the advisor misses the opportunity to gain insight into the client's circumstances through further discussions.

Fully understanding a client's income—sources, reliability, prospects, etc.—requires a deeper discussion. Here is a checklist to review with your clients to ensure you get the full picture:

1. *Sources.* The understanding of what constitutes income needs to be explored, as the sources might be beyond the client's T4—for example, income from investments, real estate, a trust set up for the benefit of the client, pension income, or spousal support payments. If the income is from a trust fund or pension plan, what are the terms? Will the trust or spousal support continue for the client's entire life, or will it end at some point?

2. *Definition.* Advisors can run into problems arising from the many definitions of income: estimated, actual, gross, net, before taxes, after taxes, income for tax-related purposes, etc. There is great confusion surrounding which definition to use for the KYC form, and the regulators have not provided guidance on this issue. While advisors are usually not required to ask for tax returns, clients suing or launching a complaint against an advisor often produce such materials to prove that the advisor failed in their regulatory and legal duty to know the client, and that the income on the KYC form was wrong.

3. *Reliability.* Is the income based on several years of employment, and so is an indication of future income? Or has it fluctuated over the past few years?

4. *Bonus or commission structure.* A close relative of reliability is the structure of the income, especially if it involves fluctuating bonuses or commissions.

5. *Shrinking or growing employer/industry.* Is the employment from which the income is derived in an industry that is thriving and expanding? Or struggling and shrinking?

6. *Income from investments.* If the client relies on income from existing investments, are these investments likely to fluctuate—e.g., speculative stocks or high-risk mutual funds? Or are they low risk, with a guaranteed income and/or return of capital? And is part of the income a return *of* capital or a return *on* capital? This distinction may impact a client's assets.

Both source and reliability of income affect your clients' ability to assume risk in the financial products they purchase, whether those are securities or insurance products. Furthermore, these factors may impact time horizon. Your client may need their investments to be liquid if their income suddenly takes a nosedive.

Advisors are required to know their clients at every stage of their relationship. Being able to substantiate the income—along with the other items on the KYC form—is crucial to avoid accusations that you failed to fulfill this regulatory and legal requirement. If there is a leveraged loan or margin used to

finance investments, the stated income is important to determine whether borrowing is a suitable strategy.

So, while you might end up with the same answer for the
income line on the KYC form—"$100,000"—don't just ask
your clients, "What is your annual income?" and leave it at
that. Down the road, you will not be in a position to prove the
accuracy of that number when challenged by a client, by the
regulator, or in court.

g. Net worth

Advisors may assume that because someone has a substantial net worth, they can take bigger risks. However, net worth
alone is not enough.

For example, your client might have substantial net worth,
but their wealth might be in serious jeopardy because of family
spending habits or lifestyle. Furthermore if the client is relatively young and neither educated nor motivated to work, then
this capital might be required to last a lifetime.

On the other hand, a client might not have substantial net
worth, but what they do have is growing due to a disciplined
plan and a long time horizon. That client might want to invest
in higher-risk investments to ensure their money grows over
their lifetime.

Net worth taken in a vacuum, without examining whether it
is growing or shrinking or whether there is a long or short time
horizon, can be misleading.

Another danger is that clients can be very private about their
net worth, making it difficult to determine their risk profile. In
this situation, it can be tempting to guess, based on such
superficial things as how the client dresses, where they live,
or what type of car they drive. Basing an estimate on any real
estate a client owns, or even their profession, might seem

more relevant, but these factors are superficial, too. The client might look the part of someone with a high net worth but may be subject to serious debt that is not disclosed. Remember, the term is "net" worth, which means assets *minus liabilities*.

I suggest that if you explore the other aspects of the KYC form, by asking the questions I provided, you will gain better insight into the client's net worth and cash flow. At the same time, you will be engaging the client in a meaningful conversation.

But what if the client clams up and refuses to share anything meaningful? When this happens, you have to make a decision. Are you willing to take on a client who is so secretive that they are preventing you from doing your job properly? If the amount of money is substantial, you may be tempted. But remember: the more secretive the client, the more risk to you. And the larger the account, the more you are exposed if there are substantial losses. High-net-worth clients tend to have lawyers already on their payroll, so the risk of a lawsuit is real. Some clients may not know their net worth. They might be completely off when they tell you the value of their assets. If this happens, you'll be left to guess, again. Yet you need this information to recommend how the client's money should be invested.

In sum, questions on the KYC form are there for a reason; engaging the client in conversations to explore them is crucial. Taking simple answers at face value will neither protect you nor your client.

Category 2: Investment knowledge
Of all the questions on the KYC form, judges and regulators tend to focus on the client's investment knowledge.[4] From

---

4   For a full analysis of client knowledge and sophistication, see *Advisor at Risk*, Chapter 6.

what I have seen, it is also the question that gets the least attention from advisors. Advisors usually show a client the options on the KYC form and ask the client which category they fall into. The client makes their choice and the advisor indicates the answer with a tick mark. The client signs the KYC form. Later, if and when the client launches a complaint against the advisor, invariably the client asserts that the information on the form is inaccurate, especially the advisor's assessment of the client's investment knowledge.

To assess your client's investment knowledge, engage them in conversation, asking about their education, whether they follow business news, and the types of investments and accounts they have had in the past. This will help you determine whether the client has the sophistication and knowledge to understand more complex products and strategies.

Category 3: Risk assessment

Until I participated in a detailed study on client risk profiles, I referred to this category as 'risk tolerance'. But after learning from academics, I now refer to the entire area of client risk as 'risk profile' or 'risk assessment'—because, as you will see below, 'risk tolerance' is only one factor of many to consider.

For example, while both real and concrete information from the client, like income and net worth, play an important role, so do emotional factors. Emotions—such as the client's perception of their financial situation, how they view the market, or how they react to market fluctuations—need to be factored in.

During my workshops, I present a chart, like the one below, and then describe certain facts and attributes from a hypothetical client case. I then ask participants which of two columns each of these facts fall into: emotional or concrete/actual.

Emotional	Concrete/Actual

HERE IS JUST such a hypothetical client fact: Jaco lost his job. Does that fact go into the emotional column, or the actual column? The answer is: it might be both. Factually, Jaco lost his job, which is a real issue. If Jaco doesn't receive another job offer, then his savings might be impacted and his risk profile might need to be amended based on this very real change. But even if Jaco secures alternative employment quickly and is not financially affected at all, his confidence might have suffered, and he might have changed his perception about his job security. That is an emotional reaction to a concrete fact. Complicated? You bet!

The emotional category is not more or less important than the concrete/actual category. But I find this exercise to be useful because it makes the advisor think through how changes in the client's situation can affect their attitude toward taking risk. Our experiences shape us, whether they are real (concrete/actual) or perceived (emotional).

B. Developing your client's risk profile

A client's risk profile is intended to be an overall determination of your client's acceptable risk level. Risk profiling permits you to identify the maximum risk your client can accept to achieve their goals. In the balance of this chapter, I explore the elements to consider when determining a client's risk profile.[5]

i. The client's willingness/unwillingness to assume risk

Sometimes advisors place too much reliance on the client's ability to ascertain what is right for themselves, and simply ask, "What is your willingness to assume risk: high, medium, or low?" This is a flawed process. Instead, I suggest asking open-ended questions about a client's attitude toward risk. Note that it is important not to influence client answers with your own biases.

Certain regulators are proponents of questionnaires, even going so far as to mandate their use.[6] But the regulators support the importance of engaging in conversation with each client, exploring the answers to any questions in a questionnaire to more fully assess the client's willingness to assume risk.

---

5   There are nine criteria for determining a client's risk profile. I have picked only six factors to briefly discuss here, so for more in-depth and academic coverage of all nine factors, along with a deeper discussion of risk in general, please read pages 5 and 6 of the report referenced in the third footnote in this chapter, available here: www.osc .gov.on.ca/documents/en/Investors/iap_20151112_risk-profiling-report.pdf.
6   See MFDA Bulletin #0611-C, "MFDA discussion paper on the use of investor questionnaires," and the sample questionnaire that accompanies it.

ii. Risk capacity

This is the financial ability of a client to endure any potential financial loss. Can the client afford to take the risk? Can they afford to experience a loss in the short term and long term? This is not a simple analysis. Yet without it, the exercise is incomplete.

iii. Loss tolerance

How much is the client prepared to lose before getting upset? People can tolerate swings as long as their account doesn't slip below a certain point. So the question is, how do you determine that point? Questions like, "If you lost more than 10% would you be upset?" can be meaningless to the client, because the number is not in dollar terms. Ask this question in dollar terms, not percentage terms. When the client indicates where their breaking point is, you can determine what percentage loss they can tolerate. It is also important to take the current market situation into account, and to point out to your clients how markets have fluctuated in the past. When markets are doing well, clients can be lulled into a false sense of comfort and may answer in a more bullish fashion than if they had just experienced a market downturn. Greed, fear, and personal experience play a significant role in the determination of a client's risk profile. It is helpful to know each client's "story" to understand and interpret their loss tolerance.

iv. Risk composure

This is about whether your client can hold it together in the face of a perceived crisis. Will they behave irrationally and seek to liquidate their investments, thereby crystallizing their loss? A crisis is not limited to a market correction; it could be a personal crisis, like losing a job or a health matter that requires expensive medical care. Advisors complain about how some clients are inclined to want to sell everything during a crisis rather than weathering the storm, as advised. If clients insist on selling at a low point, against your advice, that may be a signal that you may not have properly assessed that client's risk composure.

Risk composure, like loss tolerance, is not an easy element to test unless the client has previously experienced a crisis and can accurately describe the way they felt about it and how they reacted. If a client was in the market during a big correction and you can determine how they reacted at the time, this will help you determine this element. If the client has not weathered a market correction, then determining how they might react will be more difficult. Still, it is important to ask. Attempt to make the market correction real to the client. Tell them how much the market fell and what that would have meant, in dollar terms, to their account.

v. Risk perception

This is a close relative of risk composure. But unlike risk composure, it also is about trying to gauge a client's emotional reaction to media or to the broader economic environment. This risk may be mitigated by a client's financial literacy, education, or experience.

vi. Risk need

Risk need is the amount of risk that should be factored in for a client to meet specific financial goals, like retirement. Some advisors tend to overemphasize the importance of this criterion, particularly for clients whose goals tend to be beyond a reasonable reach. Putting too much weight on a high risk need in a client's risk profile can get you into deep trouble with regulators and judges, because the investments will invariably be unsuitable. The more out of reach a client's goal is, the higher the returns will need to be, to the point where the risk profile will be set too high. For example, if, when determining what returns are required to meet a client's financial goals, the answer is 20%, then you know that this client will have a problem meeting their needs. At this point, it is best to tell the client that this goal cannot be achieved, and that they will have to plan for less. Instead of weighting their risk need too heavily, consider all the other factors in this list, and balance risk need with loss tolerance/risk willingness and risk capacity.

Advisors sometimes feel they need to help clients who do not have enough money to retire by investing in higher-risk products than would be the case if the other criteria were properly analyzed. Here is an example of what can arise from this:

Mr. and Mrs. Shnig moved their savings from the bank to a new advisor. They told the advisor that they needed a plan that would provide them with enough money to continue their lifestyle after retirement. The clients assert that their new advisor promised to do better than what they were earning at the bank, and assured them they would have $65,000 per annum in income throughout their retirement. The Shnigs say that the advisor also cautioned that if they remained at the bank, they would run out of money by age 70, which understandably worried them.

The advisor worked backward and figured that to get them the income they needed to live comfortably from their savings for the rest of their lives, he had to put 75% of their investments into high-risk equities. The balance could be invested into a mix of lower-risk stocks or bonds. One of the investments chosen by the advisor was structured to provide the

Shnigs with a regular distribution that was a blend of a return of their own capital and income from investments that had a tax deferral benefit. The Shnigs were relieved.

However, after five years, Mr. and Mrs. Shnig began to worry again. Each time they looked at their monthly investment statement, they observed, with growing panic, that their capital was diminishing. While they needed reasonable returns to support their retirement lifestyle, they began to fear that they would run out of money. While their KYC form confirmed that they agreed to 25% medium and 75% high risk, with at least 75% in equities, Mr. and Mrs. Shnig now say they did not understand the implications. The Shnigs return to their favorite banker with their investment statement and she confirms that their risk level was set much too high.

Will a copy of the signed KYC form be sufficient evidence to support the dealer and advisor when they assert that the Shnigs had to invest aggressively, given their need for money through retirement? In this example, the Shnigs were inexperienced investors and relatively unsophisticated. So the advisor will be in the hot seat and may not fare very well. Is this the advisor's fault? What really happened was that he wanted to help the Shnigs but put himself at risk instead. Not a good idea!

With the average age of the population increasing substantially, advisors need to be on the alert for clients who have not saved enough for retirement. These clients turn to advisors to help them solve their problems, and advisors, hoping to help these clients, take on the challenge. But advisors are not magicians. Clients cannot expect advisors to always choose market winners among the many high-risk investments available.

As an advisor, you need to explain to these clients that they may have to make some serious lifestyle decisions. Advisors can only help them if the clients are prepared to step up, work with the advisors to reduce their expenses, try to increase their capital, and reduce their financial needs and expectations. But if you instead suggest that a client move from their previous advisor so you can get them the income they need, you are leading that client to believe that you are, indeed, a magician and can pull money out of thin air. You are overestimating 'risk need' over other aspects of risk.[7]

vii. *Clients will change*

I would be remiss not to mention one more aspect of setting a client's risk profile: change! Markets change, securities change, and clients change. Change can impact every other element in this list,[8] which in turn may impact a client's risk profile. That is the main reason why you need to keep in contact with clients and why dealers insist that you update your client information, and thus your KYC forms regularly.[9]

C. Boiling it down to a simple process

The client may complain that the advisor did not properly gauge their risk profile, sold them the wrong product, or both. Either way, the advisor will be in the hot seat to support their decisions with concrete evidence.

---

7   The regulators are concerned that need can overcome other aspects of suitability and be weighted too heavily, disregarding other aspects. See MFDA Bulletin #0611-C, "MFDA discussion paper on the use of investor questionnaires," and the accompanying sample questionnaire.

8   For more on the changes that can impact suitability, see *Advisor at Risk*, Chapter 4.

9   At the time of this writing, there are diverse views and rules on how often a KYC form must be updated. I suggest you check with your particular provincial regulator, SRO, and company policy manual to determine your obligations.

So how can you navigate these issues? With respect to a client's risk profile, the first step is to complete an analysis of the attributes that impact the client's risk and how these factors might affect suitability. You need to have a process to ensure constant and regular contact and communication with clients. You also need to have a process to ensure continuous documentation to reflect these communications with clients, and to know what products are available to meet the client's risk profile. It is only after all of this that you can apply your judgment to pull it all together. Put simply:

STEP 1: KYC/KYP
STEP 2: Professional judgment
STEP 3: Disclosure of product cost and risk[10]

Advisors are professionals who must go beyond the superficial to determine an accurate client profile. They do this by analyzing concrete and emotional aspects of the client's situation and perception. Only with this analysis can advisors accurately choose suitable investments. Only with evidence of this analysis can the advisor prove that the investments they chose for the client were suitable.

Summary

Suitability is one of the most complex and risky parts of the financial services industry; it forms the basis of most client

---

10   See MFDA Bulletin #0713-P, "Suitability: research paper on Canadian securities regulatory authority decisions," January 24, 2017.

complaints and litigation. Communication is a key ingredient to making an accurate determination of clients' risk profiles and being sure that clients' accounts are invested suitably.

Advisors Take Action

✓ Don't take clients' answers to KYC form questions at face value. Explore further by engaging in meaningful discussions with your clients, listening carefully, taking notes, and asking open-ended questions to determine if there is anything that might cause you to rethink their risk profile.

✓ Include both concrete information and emotional factors in each client risk profile.

✓ Complete an analysis of the attributes that impact the client's risk and how these factors might affect suitability. Be careful to not overemphasize 'risk need' over other factors of risk.

✓ Adopt a practice of constant and regular contact and communication with clients. Keep continuous documentation to reflect these communications with clients.

7

Financial Planning

―――――――――

INANCIAL PLANNING[1] HAS never been more important
than it is now, as is the need for clear communication.
Preparing a financial plan for clients is a good way to
get more information from them than you otherwise might.
It is also a good way to encourage clients to participate more
fully in planning for their future needs and goals. However,
it is impossible to build a meaningful financial plan for a client without open and detailed conversations, in which you dig
well beyond the superficial. Through this, you will gain a clear

―――――――――

1   A 'financial plan' is defined as a holistic approach that integrates financial manage-
    ment, insurance and risk management, investment planning and retirement planning,
    tax planning, and estate planning. Not everyone needs a comprehensive financial
    plan, but I suggest that everyone needs a plan to help budget and save for future needs.
    A more focused plan would include at least aspects of a comprehensive financial plan.
    In this chapter, when I refer to a 'financial plan', a 'plan', or 'financial planning', I
    mean to include all plans, from the most basic (mini) to the most comprehensive.

understanding of each client's personal story,[2] their hopes, dreams, and fears. It is only with detailed information that you can effectively conduct planning for clients.

Remember, financial planning is not a once-in-a-lifetime exercise. Clients' financial circumstances, needs, and goals change, and so must their plans. Financial plans need to be updated to ensure they reflect clients at different stages in their lives. Ongoing dialogue between advisor[3] and client will help ensure the plan continues to reflect the client's changing needs and goals. In this chapter, we will explore the importance associated with ongoing communication between advisors and clients and the risk of failing to do so in the context of financial planning. By 'dialogue', I include the need for clients to contribute with honest, forthright, and open communication. That is the reason a guide for your clients accompanies this book—so that clients understand their role.

Of course, if you are a financial planner who does not intend to have a continuing relationship with your clients, ensure this fact is set out clearly in the engagement letters and in any actual financial plans delivered to your clients.

---

2   See Chapter 4 for more on understanding a client's personal story.

3   At the time of writing, there is no regulation that requires an advisor preparing a client's financial plan to have a specific certification; however, this will likely change. Therefore, while I refer to 'advisor' within the context of the professional preparing plans, I mean someone with the training required, if not the certification, to build a financial plan. If laws change, I also mean someone with the certification required to use the title 'Planner' or 'Financial Planner'.

I. The Importance of Financial Planning

While most clients value financial planning, older clients rate it particularly highly—second only in importance to investment management.[4] But clients of all ages and life stages regularly ask their advisors questions regarding their future. Here are the questions commonly asked at each stage:

In young adult life

- "Will I ever be able to afford to buy a house/condo?"
- "Will my income permit me to live a comfortable lifestyle?"
- "How do I deal with my debt (student debt or otherwise) and how do I get myself out?"

When raising a family

- "We just had our first child and I realize that I want to take a few years and stay home instead of pursuing my career. Can we afford it with my wife being the sole breadwinner?"
- "I have lost my job. How can my family make ends meet with the sum I have saved? How long will it last us?"
- "Can we afford a second car?"
- "We want to buy a house. How much can we afford to spend?"
- "Will I be able to afford to put my children through private school? How much do I need to save each month to be able to afford that?"

---

4   From a 2015 survey published by Credo Consulting in partnership with TC Media's Investment Group of 2,002 Canadians designed to be representative of the Canadian population.

- "I had to pay for university and had a huge amount of debt after graduation. I don't want that for my children. Do I need to save for their education now? How does an RESP work?"

When nearing retirement

- "How much money do I need to save to retire by age 65 with my ongoing obligations to support my adult children and my aging parents?"
- "What age can I retire or begin working part-time?"
- "What should I do with my pension? Is it better to leave it where it is or withdraw (commute) it?"
- "If I continue to work past age 65, how will that impact my taxes?"
- "Will I be able to leave money to my children after I pass away, or will it all go to the tax man?"
- "I have helped my children with their down payments and other expenses, and now I am not sure how I can ever retire."

After retirement

- "I didn't expect to live this long. Can I maintain my lifestyle?"
- "I don't know if I am going to be healthy for many more years. Can I afford to take my children and grandchildren on a cruise?"
- "My daughter takes such good care of me. Can I afford insurance to replace her income of $55,000 until my death?"

Clients want to know what they need to earn, save, and spend to meet their financial needs and goals, regardless of what stage of life they are in. That's where financial planning comes in. Should everyone have a plan? And, if so, what are the risks of preparing financial plans to advisors and planners?

II. Risks to Advisors and Planners

There are three central risks to advisors and planners when it comes to financial planning. Let's look at each in turn.

Risk #1: Clients sue their planners

Some advisors delegate the preparation of the financial plan to a financial planner[5] within their firm. The planner should not be under the impression that since they are not the main client contact that they won't be sued or be subject to a complaint.[6]

If the planner meets with the client, they will usually give the client a business card. As well, the planner's name may be on the front of the plan document and the planner may sign the plan at the end of the document. Therefore, even if the client did not meet the planner in person, the client will likely be able to identify who the planner was.

When the client is considering who they should sue for losses, they do not hesitate to sue the planner along with the advisor and dealer. That's true even if the only service provided to the client was the preparation of a plan.

Most cases settle out of court, so it is not publicly known whether the planners had to pay any damages to complaining clients. But there are cases (like the one discussed in the following section) in which the advisors who also prepared what

---

5   This is usually someone designated as a Certified Financial Planner® (CFP) but not necessarily, as, at the time of writing, certification is not a requirement.

6   Note also that the Financial Planning Standards Council initiates its own investigations.

they refer to as a financial plan were sued for losses based on allegations concerning the plan.

Risk #2: Clients sue advisors based on the financial plan

It is also common for advisors to prepare a financial plan for the clients to whom they sell securities or insurance products. There is a reported case in which the advisors were sued based on the plan they provided. This case[7] is instructive, as it describes the events that can lead to a lawsuit, the basis of which is the preparation and delivery of, and failure to follow, a financial plan.

In this case, the clients were a married couple, Mr. and Mrs. Giesbrecht. Like many investors, they wanted to know, based on their current income, assets, liabilities, and retirement expectations, when they could afford to retire. They had a team of two advisors providing them with investment and insurance advice, and who also prepared a financial plan to help them with this question.

The Giesbrechts had done some analysis on their own, and determined they could make ends meet if they could earn $35,000 per annum from their investments from the time they retired to age 90. The Giesbrechts were in their 50s when they consulted with their two advisors. They had saved some money, and they owned their home. Their advisors analyzed the couple's financial situation and prepared a two-page letter and two pages of calculations. The letter included an introductory paragraph explaining that what followed were "some suggestions regarding your upcoming retirement..." and concluded with tables and financial charts. The letter explained

---

7   *Giesbrecht v. Canada Life Assurance Co.*, 2013 MBCA 53 (Man. CA) [*Giesbrecht* CA].

that "the attached RRIF illustration is the result of these calculations on all of these charts... we are using for the purpose of
these illustrations the assumptions as follows."[8] The assumptions used for calculations included the rate of investment
growth each year; Canada Pension Plan and Old Age Security
benefits available upon retirement; their income continuing
until retirement; the sale proceeds of their Calgary home (on
the understanding that they would rent after retirement),
which would be added to the retirement funds; and rental
costs. The advisors suggested at the conclusion of the letter
that if the clients wanted to follow the plan, then they ought to
gather together their existing savings and make additional regular deposits to their savings through a PAC (pre-authorized
contribution).

The Giesbrechts did not follow the directions in the letter
and plan but instead tucked the plan away in a drawer.

One day, soon after receiving the plan that was based on
Mr. Giesbrecht working for several more years to add to his
savings, he received a termination package from his employer,
which he accepted. He did not consult his advisors about what
impact taking the package would have on his retirement plan,
or whether he would need to get another job to ensure he
could ultimately retire in accordance with their $35,000 per
annum goal. Mrs. Giesbrecht decided to quit her job, too, also
without consulting her advisors.

They decided to retire even though they had not saved
enough money to do so and still meet their retirement spending
goal. They sold their home in Calgary. Instead of renting an

---

8   *Giesbrecht* CA, supra note 7 at para 26; Giesbrecht v. Canada Life Assurance Co., 2011
MBQB 244 at para 46 [*Giesbrecht* QB].

apartment, as contemplated in their plan, they used the proceeds of the sale to buy a home in Winnipeg to be close to their children and grandchildren.

In the years that followed, the Giesbrechts continued to maintain contact with their advisors, meeting with them regularly to get advice. Neither the Giesbrechts nor the advisors raised any issues concerning the plan and the fact that it obviously was not being followed. Neither the Giesbrechts nor the advisors—recognizing the changes in their lives—suggested that another plan should be prepared. Neither party raised the issue of whether the Giesbrechts would ultimately run out of money.

Several years after they had stopped working, Mr. and Mrs. Giesbrecht came to the realization that they would indeed run out of money. So they both went back to work. But having been out of the job market for so long, the jobs they found paid them far less than they had previously been earning. They came up with an idea: Let's sue our advisors, who had promised us comfort in our retirement years. The Giesbrechts sued the advisors, alleging misrepresentations in the plan.

At trial, the judge found in favor of the Giesbrechts. The judge awarded them damages based on several years' loss of income, concluding that the advisors failed to fulfill their obligations to the Giesbrechts both before and after their retirement.

I was really surprised by this finding when I read the decision. The judges of the Manitoba Court of Appeal appeared to agree with me, because they overturned the trial judge's decision. The findings of the Court of Appeal echoed my thoughts. How could the advisors be held responsible for the losses when:

a. the Giesbrechts' own evidence was that they didn't rely on the plan at all, including for their decision to retire;[9]
b. the Giesbrechts did not consult with their advisors before they retired to determine whether they were on track to fund $35,000 per year for the rest of their lives, as contemplated;[10] and
c. the Giesbrechts admitted that they didn't deposit their savings or the proceeds from the sale of their home, key assumptions in their plan?[11]

Further, the examples of different scenarios found in the schedule to the plan were described as 'illustrations', based on a number of assumptions that were also set out in the plan. None of this was interpreted by the Court of Appeal to be representations by the advisors upon which the clients could reasonably assert they relied; these were not guarantees.[12] The actions taken by the Giesbrechts to stop working and to sell their house and buy another one were not contemplated in the plan. Therefore, the Court of Appeal reversed the trial judge's findings on the basis that the lower court's analysis that the advisors were responsible for the damages was flawed.[13]

However, as a litigator, I know that even when advisors win, they really lose, because of the energy and resources spent to defend the action and the subsequent appeal. Even if the advisors had errors and omissions insurance (E&O) for themselves,

---

9   *Giesbrecht QB, ibid* at para 50.
10 *Giesbrecht QB, supra* note 8 at paras 53–54.
11 *Giesbrecht CA, supra* note 7 at para 16; *Giesbrecht QB, supra* note 8 at para 48.
12 *Giesbrecht CA, supra* note 7 at para 42.
13 *Giesbrecht CA, supra* note 7 at para 91.

the respective companies under which they operated were also sued and may not have had separate entity E&O. If this was the case, the companies may have had to pay for part of the defense of the action. Even if there was E&O for all parties being sued, there are substantial hidden costs associated with the distraction and stress resulting from protracted litigation in which an advisor's reputation is on the line. The most troubling part of this case is that both advisors were retired throughout this litigation.[14] Litigation was commenced in 2004 and judgment was rendered by the Court of Appeal on June 10, 2013. Almost ten years of their retirement was spent dealing with this case. They won, but, really, they lost.

So what can advisors and planners learn from this court decision?

i.   Clear communication is key before the plan is prepared

The purpose of a plan is that it is a living document. This means clients must be honest with themselves and transparent with their advisors about debts, liabilities, goals, objectives, and any competing interests. The Giesbrechts had competing interests: they wanted to stop working immediately and spend more time with their children and grandchildren, but they couldn't afford to do that for several more years.

ii.   Communication needs to continue after delivery of the plan to the client

We all know it is an advisor's duty to know their client at every stage of their relationship to ensure investments are adjusted

---

14   *Giesbrecht* QB, supra note 8 at para 58, 59.

as clients change.[15] This concept applies equally to financial planning; plans must continue to be updated as the client changes and evolves. There are endless reasons why a client's needs might change:

1. They met their goals and need to establish new ones.
2. Their financial situation changed to render the previously set goals impossible to achieve.
3. The client's values and circumstances, and therefore needs, changed due to life events.

It is important to explore these changes through continuing dialogue with your clients. Ask probing questions and build trust to ensure they share all pertinent information. Further, as your clients change, so must their plan to reflect their new circumstances and goals.

iii. Is this a continuing obligation or a one-time plan?

Include language in both the letter of engagement and in the plan itself that indicates whether this is a one-time, point-in-time plan, for which the planning mandate is over after it is delivered, or if there is a continuing relationship. If it is a one-time plan, the client must be advised that it is not intended that there will be any follow-up to revise the plan to reflect future changes. If it is a continuing relationship, emphasize the client's obligation to communicate their personal changes to you.

Clients and advisors need to discuss what impact different types of personal changes might have on the plan that will

---

15   Investment fund managers: please refer to National Instrument 31-103, "Registration Requirements, Exemptions and Ongoing Registrant Obligations, Part 13: Dealing with clients—individuals and firms," sections 13.2 and 13.3.

result in the need for an update. This provision was not contained in the Giesbrechts' plan. Indeed, the Giesbrechts didn't discuss their termination of employment and early retirement with the advisors. However, the advisors didn't raise the terms of the plan and the changes they were aware of with the Giesbrechts, either. The advisors failed to ask follow-up questions, like how the Giesbrechts intended to fund their early retirement, having moved to Winnipeg years before their plan accounted for such a move. This should have resulted in the advisors confirming in writing that their plan was out of date and that the Giesbrechts were surely not going to achieve the goals set out in the plan. It was this communication failure, on both sides, that led to the litigation.

iv. Carefully choose the language and messages
What you say and how you say it is very important in any financial plan. Here are some specific things to be mindful of:

1. Ensure the plan is clearly developed and explained in writing. I have seen many different (template) plans, and many have been difficult to understand and digest. Longer is not necessarily better.

2. Make sure the language used is clear. Avoid jargon or acronyms that the client might not understand.

3. If there are any 'assumptions' and 'illustrations', as opposed to reliable facts, these should be clearly indicated as such.

4. Remember, the credibility of the witnesses affects trial judges, the OBSI, and regulators, who hear your version of

events as well as the client's. In the Giesbrecht case, the judges questioned whether the clients were as unsophisticated as they portrayed themselves at trial. The trial judge concluded that the Giesbrechts did indeed have sufficient understanding of their plan and the assumptions set out therein.[16]

5. Don't use a minuscule font in a footnote or otherwise to express terms that may seem unimportant. If a term is in the plan, don't undervalue it through formatting or footnotes.

6. Discuss the plan with the client. Don't just deliver a written plan. This is an opportunity to connect and build the client relationship while ensuring the client understands the plan, the assumptions (which might change), and the need to update you if anything changes in their life. The more engaged the client is, the more likely the client will follow your advice, and the path set out in the plan.

v. *Understand, and meet, the standards to which you will be held*

Even if you do not have a planning designation from any of the authorities,[17] such as the Financial Planning Standards Council (FPSC), you could still be held to their standards. In the Giesbrecht case, both the *Conduct and Practices Handbook* (or CPH) and the FPSC Rules of Conduct were referred to and considered for guidance on the standards required of planners, as well as on what is reasonably expected in a financial

---

16   *Giesbrecht* QB, supra note 8 at para 16–18, 48–51.

17   The rules may change, compelling planners to obtain a designation.

plan.[18] This was despite the fact that the CPH course is not actually law and the two advisors in the Giesbrecht case did not have a planning certification or designation.

vi. Don't blindly use a template

If you use a template or software program, be sure to not blindly accept what is in that template or plan. Ask yourself what applies and what doesn't, as well as what might be missing in the template that could be necessary to capture the client's unique situation.

If the client does not want to embark on the preparation of a full, comprehensive financial plan but is interested to know, loosely, the answer to certain planning questions like those at the beginning of this chapter, consider whether a letter, or 'mini-plan', could be more appropriate. Ensure the language of the letter or mini-plan are checked to confirm there are no guarantees and that any number crunching is clearly indicated on the plan document to be just for illustration purposes. Further, if a full, comprehensive plan is not prepared, put what is and is not included into the engagement letter, and then state it again in the mini-plan itself. That will avoid any miscommunication and reduce the risk that a client will later suggest that you didn't fulfill your duty.

vii. Clearly set out any limitations to the financial plan

If there are time or other limitations that would affect the plan's usefulness, set them out clearly, rather than hiding them in a minuscule font or in a footnote. Again, if your relationship with the client is not one of advisor but strictly as a one-time planner, be certain to put any and all limitations to

---

18   *Giesbrecht* QB, supra note 8 at para 126–127, 133.

the relationship and service provided in writing, both in the initial engagement letter and in the plan itself.

Risk #3: The documents are incomplete

In certain organizations, there is supervision of the planning function and of the planners' work. However, in other organizations, the supervision is inconsistent or nonexistent. Regardless of whether you have someone supervising your planning function or not, ensure that the planning documents are correct, complete, consistent, and customized (rather than cookie-cutter), and that there is regular communication with the clients that is carefully documented.

What do each of those things involve? Here is a checklist:

1. *Correct.* Consider the following:

   a. *Quality of information communicated:* Was the information delivered to the person preparing the financial plan orally or in writing? How reliable is it? If it is an advisor passing along information to the planner, does the advisor really know his client?

   b. *Accuracy:* Is the client in tune with their personal goals? Is the client being transparent about their personal information? Does the client even know all the personal information required? Is the client providing reliable information or just "best guess" numbers that should not be relied upon for planning purposes? If you rely on information provided by the client that has not been independently verified, ensure you state this clearly in the plan. For example, if the client tells you to rely on assumptions that certain assets have a certain value, ensure you specify that these are only assumptions and have not been independently verified.

c. *Up-to-date:* If out-of-date information is being relied upon, then the statements, assumptions, or conclusions found in the plan may not be accurate, either.

d. *Originating documents:* You might want to verify the accuracy of what clients say with documents like their credit card statements or bank records to show the actual expenses the client incurs regularly.

2. **Complete.** Sometimes the planner doesn't receive a complete picture from the client of their financial situation during the planning meetings. The advisor, who works with the clients more regularly, may obtain additional information, which might affect the plan. The advisor needs to convey this full picture to the planner. Here are some other issues to consider:

a. *History:* Is it sufficient to obtain a snapshot of the client's present financial situation? It would be better to also get a complete history of the client so that the planner can consider the direction in which the client's circumstances are trending. For example, it would be helpful for the planner to know if the client is increasing or decreasing their debt burden as they are making more money. If the client will be increasing their debt, then that needs to be planned for. If the client is decreasing their debt, then the client may need less savings for retirement. Historic information is important for the planner to assess the client's future needs.

b. *Privacy concerns:* Clients can be private about their personal financial situation.[19] Therefore, the planner needs to explain to the client the importance of obtaining an accurate and up-to-date financial picture, as well as the steps the planner takes to keep such information secure from the view of others.

c. *Integration:* Does the planner integrate all the information provided (the good, bad, and ugly) into the plan?

d. *Scenarios:* Does the plan include different scenarios? Are there different scenarios for a plan between two people, such as life partners or spouses, in which one plans to retire before the other? Do the different scenarios encompass a reasonable range of possibilities, such as the stock market underperforming or the client's income not increasing in certain years? Does the plan include a conservative/balanced approach? Will a third person reviewing it (regulator or judge) think it makes sense and is sound?

3. **Consistent.** Ensuring consistency in a plan has many steps:

a. *More people, more inconsistencies:* Does the planner examine information and materials received from the advisor to ensure they are consistent with information obtained directly from the client? If the advisor is preparing the plan, is the information previously obtained from the client consistent with information received for the plan? If the plan is being prepared for a couple, married or

---

19   See the client guide at the end of this book, which is available for download online, to help bridge the communication gap with clients with privacy concerns.

life-partners, is the plan consistent with information and documentation provided by both people? If there are disconnects, these must be discussed with both people to determine how the inconsistences can be reflected in the plan. Once a financial plan is prepared, go back and review all the materials collected, especially the KYC form and the advisor's notes, to ensure the materials are consistent. Here are a couple of examples:

- *Time horizon:* Is the time frame within which the client may need access to their funds in the KYC consistent with the client's financial plan? If the KYC indicates the time horizon is 10 years or more and the plan indicates an intention to buy a home in three years, then the KYC might be wrong (unless the funds in the account are not for the purpose of the home purchase).

- *Income, assets, liabilities:* The income, assets, and liabilities in the KYC may not be as up-to-date as the plan or vice versa. These should be consistent. If these are not in sync, there may be allegations that either the plan is not up to standard or the KYC has not been updated. Either way, the advisor may be called to the hot seat.

b. *Gaps:* Once a financial plan is prepared, go back and review all the materials collected. Are there gaps between information/documentation and the plan? These need to be investigated, identified, explored with the client, and resolved if possible. If a gap cannot be resolved, it should be noted in the plan so that it will not later be interpreted to be an oversight by the planner.

c. *Dig deep:* Dig down and through all documentation, beyond the information previously obtained. Inconsistent information obtained from the client or from the servicing advisor (e.g., KYC information or answers to questionnaires) can be evidence of the advisor not asking the right questions, the client not understanding the questions, or the planner not investigating the reason for the inconsistency.

d. *Paper trail:* This may be required if there are inconsistent facts. For example, a client might say they want to retire at age 55 but has not saved for this purpose. Any explanations of inconsistencies should be documented so that the planner is not later accused of miscommunicating to the client, like in the Giesbrecht case.

4. **Customized.** Watch out for plan-preparation methods that fall short in customizing a plan for a particular client. These include:

a. *Computer programmed plans:* I have seen the use of a computer program result in plans that are not flexible in presentation, format, or content. Computer generated templates are fine, but the information needs to be customized for each client. Furthermore, you need to understand whether there are assumptions built into the software, what these are, and whether they apply in the circumstances of the particular client.

b. *Cookie-cutter plans:* A plan that is too generic can be a signal to a judge or regulator that you did not put sufficient thought into the plan. This will be obvious if there is more than one complaining client and they both (or all) have the identical template. You need to carefully review the end product to ensure the plan is applicable to the client, and does not rely too heavily on precedent or software programs.

5. **Communicated.** Finally, here are some finer points of communication that you need to add to your checklist:

   a. *Communication style:* Simple explanations are required for less sophisticated clients. Some clients understand pie charts and graphs well, but others find them complex. Ensure the ultimate written plan you deliver is adapted to the client's ability to understand.

   b. *Meetings:* Supporting the written plan with an in-person meeting can improve the client's understanding. This is also an opportunity to emphasize that the client knows that projections are simply that, and not guarantees. Review all of these aspects of the plan to reduce the chances of mistakes and disappointed clients.

   c. *Bring on more eyes:* If the plan is not prepared by the investing advisor, a third-party supervisor can help identify any inconsistencies that need to be flagged to ensure the financial plan is followed by the advisor. This will help protect the client, the advisor, and the financial planner.

III. How Do You Reduce Your Planning Risk?

The risks to providing a financial plan to a client may seem considerable, but there are steps advisors can take to protect themselves and their team—and, in doing so, their client as well.

A. Take a step back and consider

Did you get an accurate picture of the client's financial situation? Does it all make sense and hang together nicely? Plans are not just about dollars and cents. To prepare a plan that is going to help the client meet their goals, the planner needs to understand the client's values, expectations, goals, fears, and needs.

B. Think it through

How will you deliver the messages in the plan? Here are some things to consider:

1. *Manage client expectations when you present the plan.* This will not be the first or last time this is mentioned in this book, but I would be remiss not to reemphasize the importance of this step in the planning process. Clients are planning for the next steps and stages of life, whether that be a large purchase or retirement. If it will take longer than expected for them to achieve their goals (e.g., to buy a house or to retire), better they know sooner rather than later. Expectations need to be managed so the client is aware of their role in meeting their goals. Clients sue when they are surprised, so managing expectations when the financial plan is delivered is key.

2. *Review the financial plan with the client.* Do this in a way that ensures they understand any assumptions set out in the plan. If the assumptions don't work out, then the plan will have to be adjusted. The client needs to know this is part of the process. The planners in the Giesbrecht case should have made this clear at the outset and followed up when they knew that the clients were not following the plan.

3. *Clients and advisors/planners are partners.* Ensure the clients understand that they need to fulfill their part of the bargain. If clients want to achieve their goals, they must step up to the plate and do what needs to be done. If this is not clearly communicated when the plan is delivered, then clients may not get the message that clients and advisors need to work as partners. If clients have an obligation to take certain steps to meet goals set out in their plan, this has to be clearly set out in their plan, as well as communicated orally and followed up on. For example, if a client needs tax or legal advice, make sure this is clearly set out in the engagement letter and/or the plan document. The clearer you delineate which responsibilities are yours and which are the client's, the more likely these tasks will be fulfilled and the plan carried out, which in turn will reduce the risk of disappointment and litigation.

C. Think of the plan as a living and breathing document

The client needs to understand that to reflect a person's life changes, planning must be a process. What does this mean?

1. Financial plans need to change as clients change. The plan will need to be adjusted for different life events (e.g., paying

for a wedding, losing a job, or getting a big bonus). Any financial situation that impacts the plan must be updated in both the KYC form and in the plan itself. Even if the client doesn't report any substantial changes, you need to have a system that serves to remind you that the plan needs to be reviewed for a possible update. People's circumstances change more frequently than they did decades ago. They may marry more than once and change jobs, and even careers, more often. So be mindful of the potential and actual changes.

2. ***Short-term pain for long-term gain.*** Remind clients of the impact of their short-term decisions (e.g., buying a car they really want) on their long-term goals (e.g., buying a house). Don't be afraid to remind them and then put it in writing. Clients have selective memories. They may point to the "promises" in the plan, and ignore how they failed to take the steps needed to fulfill their goals. Financial plans have clauses that remind the client that these are not promises but goals to be achieved based on certain assumptions. Even so, clients need to be reminded.

3. ***Record any red flags.*** If clients are irresponsible with their money and this throws them off their plan, put these issues in writing. Remind them that they are making choices that are inconsistent with their long-term goals. The plan will need to be adjusted, depending on what the client does to fulfill their part of the equation. It is the responsibility of the planner/advisor to ensure this is accomplished and clearly communicated to clients.

Summary

Clients want to know how to meet their financial goals. To build a meaningful financial plan for clients, advisors need to engage in open and detailed conversations with clients, keeping their plans updated to reflect changes in client circumstances. In the context of financial planning, maintaining ongoing communication between you and your clients is of utmost importance, given the risks of failing to do so.

Advisors Take Action

✓ Ask probing questions and build trust with your clients so they share all pertinent information. Use continuing dialogue to explore changes in your clients' circumstances and goals; update their plans accordingly. Have a system in place to remind you that each plan needs to be reviewed periodically for a possible update.

✓ Include language in both the letter of engagement and in the plan itself to indicate any and all limitations to the relationship and service provided. Advise your client of the implications of any such limitations.

✓ Always ensure that planning documents are correct, complete, consistent, current, and customized and that there is regular and carefully documented communication with your clients.

✓ Manage client expectations so that your clients understand their role in communicating with you and carrying out their plan.

8

Women Clients

WOMEN CLIENTS[1] HAVE become a major area of growth in the financial advisory industry. Here is why: more women are managing their own wealth because they are single, divorced, better educated, and in more senior and better-paying jobs than previous generations. Also, the average age of the population is increasing. Men often pass away before their wives, leaving women to manage their financial affairs on their own. Advisors who overlook this shift are simply missing a huge opportunity.[2] So how should advisors— men or women—approach women clients? There have been

---

1   While much of this chapter might also apply to male clients, I urge you to read it addressing your mind to women clients.

2   "If not making a significant effort to attract women clients to your practice, you're missing out on a great business-growth opportunity"—from "How to attract women clients," by JoAnne Sommers, July 7, 2014, *Investment Executive*.

studies indicating that women's relationship with money and the manner in which they prefer to be approached may be different from men.

I. Why Women Are Important, in Case You Don't Already Know!

Women's share of the economy represents the largest emerging pool of wealth on the horizon because of three trends: 1) more women are working; 2) women have become more involved in family finances; and 3) more women are inheriting wealth, owing to their longevity.[3] It would be unwise to consider women a niche market. Women are not a market segment but a huge portion of the population.

Perhaps, though, you'd like to target a particular subgroup of women. Before you launch a marketing campaign, consider what studies have been written about women and investing. Only after thinking about the impact of this information can you ask yourself how you might approach this opportunity. What will you do to mitigate the potential risks associated with servicing or, worse, neglecting the female population?

What do I mean by neglecting the female population? Here is an example of how things went wrong for one advisor who overlooked his client's spouse.

The advisor has an appointment with his clients, Mr. and Mrs. Bunny, who have their own accounts with the advisor,

---

3   I suggest you read the entirety of: Michal J. Silverstein, Kosuke Kato, and Pia Tischerhauserall, "Women want more (in financial services)," Boston Consulting Group, 2009, and Peter Damisch, Monish Kumar, Anna Zakrzewski, and Natalia Zhiglinskaya, "Leveling the playing field," Boston Consulting Group, 2010.

as well as a joint account. They are meeting the advisor to update their KYC forms for all of the accounts and review their financial plans. Mr. Bunny shows up and tells the advisor that Mrs. Bunny is waiting downstairs in the car. They should go ahead without her. The advisor, fearful of being too insistent that Mrs. Bunny attend, proceeds with the meeting. When they are finished talking, he hands over the KYC forms for Mr. and Mrs. Bunny to sign for each of their accounts. Mr. Bunny signs and tells the advisor to wait a few minutes while he goes to the car to get Mrs. Bunny to sign. The advisor suspects that Mrs. Bunny is not really in the car and Mr. Bunny is going to sign for her. Yet the advisor doesn't say anything when Mr. Bunny returns a few minutes later with the signed forms. The advisor accepts the forms as authentic and proceeds to take additional investment instructions from Mr. Bunny for his account, his wife's account, and their joint account. The advisor doesn't compare the signature on the new documents with the previous ones he has on file, to verify that it is Mrs. Bunny's signature. There is no trading authority permitting instructions to come from Mr. Bunny for Mrs. Bunny's account. Later, after years of trading on all accounts, with instructions coming only from Mr. Bunny, the account plummets in value. Both Mr. and Mrs. Bunny sue for their losses. Mrs. Bunny alleges that her account was traded on a discretionary basis and that the advisor was remiss in his obligation to know her as a client.

This is a shocking example of how some wives have been kept out of the picture. While I hope this is changing, I am not sure all advisors appreciate that this has to stop immediately— particularly if they have any intention of expanding this area of their business—and avoid risking their reputation and facing the possibility of a severe penalty.

II. What Is the Opportunity?

Here are a few very specific reasons for advisors to pay serious attention to this segment of the population.

A. Women's wealth is growing

A recent newspaper ad illustrates how important women are becoming to the investment industry. It depicted a woman client with a male investment advisor perched on her shoulder, tapping away on his laptop.

To me, this ad was confirmation that securities dealers are waking up to the substantial wealth Canadian women control. This number is reported to be around $3.2 trillion, according to research from Investor Economics Inc.[4]

So why was the advisor in the image a man? While this isn't hard fact, the *Globe and Mail* reported recently that men comprise about 80–85% of financial advisors at banks and wealth management firms, and that while banks and other financial service firms are attempting to recruit more women, the growth has been very slow.[5] BMO reports an increase of just one percentage point since 2012. It has been suggested that women are more inclined to prefer salaried positions over commission-based ones. The few firms I have encountered that do not have a commission-based model have no shortage of women advisors. However, when you look at other industries upon which remuneration is based on commission,

---

4   "Time, treasure, talent: Canadian women and philanthropy," a study published by TD and Investor Economics; available at www.td.com/ca/documnt/PDF/tdw-pgf-canadian-women-and-philanthropy.pdf.

5   Jacqueline Nelson, "The changing face of wealth," Globe and Mail, August 9, 2014.

like real estate agents, there also appears to be no shortage of women. So I am not sure why there are so few women advisors.

Even if you are a woman advisor, pay close attention to this chapter because you might be inclined to believe you understand women better than your male counterparts—and you might be wrong. Why? Because assuming that most women think like you is a preconception that is best resisted. The wants and needs of your women clients may be very different from your own.

What do the statistics tell us? According to research commissioned by the TD Bank, 90% of Canadian women will have total control over their finances at some point in their lives.[6] In addition, a recent report from the Boston Consulting Group suggests that one-third of North American women earn more than their husbands.[7] While the median real wage (adjusted for inflation) was flat in Canada over the five years before the result of this study, men's wages actually fell while women enjoyed modest gains.[8] Even more significant is that the median wage for women increased by 24% from 1980 to 2011, while the median wage for men fell 14%.[9]

As reported in the *Globe and Mail*,[10] Canada's six major banks and Canada's largest life insurers are becoming more aggressive when it comes to the wealth management sector. As control of assets shifts to women, and their median income increases, they will continue to be given more emphasis in the advertising budgets of dealers and insurance companies.

---

6   TD and Investor Economics. "Time, treasure, talent."
7   Silverstein et al., "Women want more (in financial services)."
8   Statistics Canada as reported by David Parkinson, "For wage earners, it's increasingly a woman's world," Globe and Mail, October 9, 2014.
9   *Ibid.*
10   Nelson, "The changing face of wealth."

B. Women make referrals

Studies have shown that women make plenty of referrals. "Over a lifetime, women will make 26 referrals to their financial advisor on average, compared with 11 by the typical male client," says Kathleen Burns Kingsbury, a wealth psychology expert and author of *How to Give Financial Advice to Women*. "If you do the right things, and in a way that fosters trust in female clients, they will connect you with their friends."[11]

Whether it is to recommend a good supplier for something needed for our homes, a professional advisor, or a great restaurant, my girlfriends and I are an important resource for each other. Although you may have heard of "the men's club," you may not have heard about "the women's club." Those of you who have attended my presentations on seniors might remember the photograph of the three women, likely over 80, in colorful bathing caps, all smiling. These women look alert. They know how to take care of themselves. They have each outlived their husbands. Even before their husbands died, these women were well informed, following the news every day and doing their own banking. They are a referral network for each other.

Here's another interesting finding: according to recent research from the US-based Spectrem Group Inc., 70% of women change their advisor within one year of their husband's death.[12] So there will be many widowed, older women, changing their advisors. Advisors need to understand how to

---

11 Andrew Osterland, "Female clients more likely than men to make referrals," *Investment News*, April 24, 2012.

12 "Women and wealth: the changing face of wealth in Canada and its implications for advisors," report commissioned by IPC Wealth (Strategic Insight), as reported by Advisor.ca, September 7, 2017.

get those referrals. I have referred many people to my advisor—I cannot say exactly how many, but I am on track for 26 in my lifetime, for sure!

C. You can change your practice to include women clients

When meeting with a married male client about his joint account, be sure to include his wife. While I feel a bit ill having to say this, she is your client, too. It is your legal, regulatory, and beyond obligation to treat her the same as her husband.[13] Don't allow Mrs. Bunny to be left in the car or at home. Make sure she is attending meetings with you, with or without her husband. Be one of the advisors whom the 30% of recent widows stick with and refer to their networking group.

Because it is easier to find new clients through existing ones, I suggest you take every existing woman client you may have had playing a subordinate role, and move them to center stage. If you become a trusted advisor to your woman clients, they will not let you go when their spouse dies.

Speaking from personal experience, my advisor is like my business partner. I consult her on every personal financial decision I make. I don't make a decision that may impact my taxes, income, cash flow, or insurance without her. When I had to deal with RESPs, I turned to her, too. She has grown children and could guide me based on her knowledge and experience. She is also my cheerleader. When I hit financial milestones, she is right there applauding me. If you become that type of advisor to your women clients, they will rely on you even more and never leave you.

---

13   Nelson, "The changing face of wealth."

II. What Are the Risks?

As advisors become more aware of the importance of serving women clients, they need to ensure they avoid making some common mistakes. That means serving women clients properly. Here is a list and analysis of common risks that I have observed.

A. Invisible clients

By allowing Mr. Bunny to run the show, his advisor committed the following infractions:

1. Failure to know his client.
2. Accepting one client's signature for another.[14]
3. Accepting trading instructions without documentation.

Just because it was Mr. Bunny's idea that Mrs. Bunny not attend the meeting doesn't mean Mr. Bunny won't later sue his advisor or support Mrs. Bunny's complaint.[15]

Advisors are sometimes lax with the rules when it is the client's idea, particularly if it is a familiar client. Advisors

---

14 Signing for someone else is never permitted, even when there is permission granted. The only thing permitted is a trading authority or power of attorney, neither of which permits someone to sign another person's name. Any signatures required from the person with trading authority or POA would be their own signatures and not the signature of the person from whom the authority is given. Section 13.2 of National Instrument (NI) 31-103, among other things, requires registrants to take reasonable steps to establish the identity of a client, and to ensure that they have sufficient information to meet suitability obligations. Under section 13.2(4) of NI 31-103, registrants are required to make reasonable efforts to keep their clients' KYC information current.

15 Mrs. Bunny might sue on her own if she divorces or becomes widowed, especially after she receives advice from another advisor in respect of the losses.

tend to believe that clients with whom they have become well acquainted would never complain or sue. These advisors are gravely mistaken. I have represented many advisors against clients they thought they knew well. I can assure you that most advisors are surprised when the Mr. and Mrs. Bunnys of the world sue, especially if they are friends or relatives.

Allowing Mr. Bunny to call the shots puts the advisor's reputation and license at risk. It is also a missed opportunity to develop a relationship with Mrs. Bunny. If a Mr. Bunny does bring a Mrs. Bunny to a meeting, be sure to address Mrs. Bunny as often as you do Mr. Bunny. Ask her questions that allow you to later prove you knew her. Take an interest in her and what she thinks. Don't think for a moment that she likes to be ignored, even if her husband seems more engaged in the process than she is. If you ignore her, be prepared to receive transfer-out papers if she and Mr. Bunny separate or divorce or if Mr. Bunny passes away.[16]

B. Generalizing from one woman to all women

Be careful not to paint all women with the same brush. There are as many different types of women as men. Besides, it can be offensive to anyone to be stereotyped.

Worse, it would be a regulatory and legal violation for an advisor to fail to get to know any client before investing their money, regardless of whether that client is male or female. Generalizing, instead of taking the time to know each client, could not only lead to a legal and regulatory infraction, it is also a huge marketing mistake. Knowing each client, and each client's attitude toward risk, is crucial.

---

16 For more on treating a woman like "the invisible client," see *Advisor at Risk*, Chapter 8.

Consider this advice from "Leveling the playing field," a 2010 study by the Boston Consulting Group: "Many women told us that their gender should have no bearing on the advice they receive. In truth, however, female clients often share some important characteristics. Private banks should focus on these common traits, but not to the exclusion of individual characteristics... women tend to focus on long-term objectives, and to value the big picture view more than the technical aspects of individual products. [Advisors] should keep these characteristics in mind."[17] I suggest you read this study in full. The takeaway: avoid stereotypes, but address commonalities.

Here are two more recommendations from the Boston Group's study:

1. Cater to the client, not the gender. "The communication style should be determined on a case-by-case basis and should acknowledge the wide array of client profiles."

2. Show empathy and build trust. "Female clients are likely to value these qualities more than men do. Advisors need to listen to the client and always keep her overarching objectives front and center. Private banking is, after all, a people business."

In their book, *Never Be Closing*, authors and sales experts Tim Hurson and Tim Dunne state that unless you understand people and their problems, you will never understand how to help solve them. The more you learn about their situation, the better you can help them. According to Hurson and Dunne, selling is all about helping people. Their advice is to take the

---

17   Damisch,"Leveling the playing field," page 9.

time to understand each client. Only then will you understand how to serve them properly.[18]

Interestingly, 85% of the women surveyed by the Boston Consulting Group reported being indifferent to the gender of their advisor. They cared more about the advisor's personality, qualifications, and getting the best person for the job.

When it comes to marketing to women, men aren't the only ones who might get it wrong. Women advisors, too, may presume too much.

One day, a fancy package arrived at my office from a woman advisor seeking my business. In the package was a small, black evening bag, with a card introducing the advisor and inviting me to call her to meet. I do not remember if she followed up with a telephone call.

I assume she was targeting me because, as a lawyer, I was a potential high-net-worth client. I wondered how many high-net-worth women would have appreciated receiving a black evening bag, or whether most already had at least one. I also wondered whether her market research indicated this would be an effective tool or whether she just assumed.

Presumably, this little package and the courier delivery were expensive. It might have been a good idea in that I remembered the gesture. She may have attracted women clients who were ready to explore changing their advisor. Now, my advisor at the time wasn't meeting my needs. Yet I was not inclined to meet with the advisor who sent me the evening bag.

I should have been open to the idea of another advisor who provided more of a full service. But the gift of the evening bag, for some reason, didn't intrigue me. Maybe because the evening bag didn't convey that the advisor understood me or my

---

18 Hurson and Dunne, *Never Be Closing*.

needs. I wonder if, instead, she had somehow determined that as a busy career woman, I needed a more holistic service than I might have been getting. She could have reached out to me, explaining how her services would have included managing my registered plans. Perhaps then I would have met with her and maybe given her my business. As it was, though, I didn't even keep her card or contact information for another day.

While that marketing didn't influence me, it might very well have influenced some women.[19] Others, though, might have found it patronizing.[20]

For my part, I would have preferred something more thought-provoking, acknowledging my needs as a mother, lawyer, and woman, an extremely hard worker who didn't have time to manage her own financial affairs. I wasn't particularly in need of an evening bag but rather of services that would make my life easier. I needed an advisor who would make sure I contributed to my RESP and RRSP each year. The gift didn't give me a sense that this advisor was gearing up to help solve my problems.

As the Boston Consulting Group states, "an initiative aimed explicitly at women is only going to scratch the surface of a client's needs. Many other factors, such as the client's stage in life and in work... and her level of wealth, come into play."[21] The differences among individuals are going to be far more important than the differences between genders.

---

19 Perhaps if she reads this book, she will call me and inform me as to the success of that marketing effort.
20 Damisch et al., "Leveling the playing field."
21 *Ibid*, page 10.

Many advisors find that seminars are an excellent way to reach out to clients—both women and men. Does it make sense to do a seminar for women? Yes, but be sure you don't assume that all women will react to the message in the same way. Women are not a homogeneous group. The Boston Group suggests it might be enough to fine-tune the seminar for women clients.[22] Do your homework, understand the particular segment of women you aim to service, and consider how best to proceed. Be cautious not to just wrap a pink ribbon around it and think it will appeal to women.

C. Sophistication

Determining a client's sophistication is incredibly important. The challenge for advisors is to determine whether the client is:

- experienced and knowledgeable, and whether the money was earned on her own, inherited, or from insurance proceeds;
- experienced but unwilling to deal with her advisor, perhaps due to age or illness;
- inexperienced, but willing and able to learn;
- inexperienced, able, but unwilling to learn; or
- inexperienced, unable, and unwilling to learn.[23]

i. Don't judge too quickly

It may not be obvious into which category each woman you meet fits. You need to get to know them individually to figure

---

22 *Ibid*, page 1.

23 Sometimes, mental capacity issues can render a client unable to learn, but this is not unique to women and not the subject of this chapter.

this out. This may be easier said than done. For example, Mrs. Jacuberry has stayed at home while her husband built a business from the ground up, eventually achieving an enterprise that they were ultimately able to take public. Without asking, you wouldn't know that she did the bookkeeping and kept the records for her husband's company right up to the company's IPO. Because her husband was so busy with the business, she was also responsible for all the family finances and budgeting.

But even if a woman's husband is the one who handles the finances, don't underestimate her ability to understand your explanations. You need to make sure she understands the alternatives before her so she can make informed choices. That is your regulatory and legal obligation.

Women might be inclined to understate their level of investment sophistication.[24] Studies show that women lack confidence when it comes to the topic of investing, and they can sometimes use the excuse that the topic is too personal as a way to avoid the discussion.[25] Advisors have the challenging task of figuring out how much women clients really understand, and how they can encourage women to share private information, particularly if such reluctance is based on a

---

24 "Do men and women have different savings habits?" Financial Independence Hub, December 5, 2017; see also Statistics Canada data in "For wage earners, it's increasingly a women's world"; Parkinson, "For wage earners"; when Statistics Canada quizzed Canadians who rated themselves as financially literate, one in every three women failed the literacy test, while one in every four men failed. Further, 25% of both men and women who expressed insecurity in their financial literacy came close to acing the quiz, indicating that confident people overstate their knowledge whereas less confident people understate it. Both genders are bad at self-assessment.

25 Sandy Betner Chaikin, "Women and investing: Is investing too personal?", Nasdaq Inc., December 4, 2017.

confidence issue. This is accomplished by asking the relevant questions, in a manner that is sensitive to this insecurity.

ii. Ask thoughtful questions

You could ask a woman client how they have budgeted for their expenses; what they look for when they review their bank or investment statements; what interests them if and when they read or watch the news; or what their views are about investing, the stock market, mutual funds, bonds, or exchange traded funds.

Keep a strong paper trail of what the client tells you and whether you think they understand or not. Also, note whether they are willing to admit that they don't understand something or whether they seem embarrassed to admit it. On the flip side, try to determine if they are actually more knowledgeable than they are letting on.

iii. Clients may not be as you think they are

An advisor might think that, as a lawyer with expertise in the advisor/dealer industry, I have a good understanding of complicated products. But if you begin to spout off information about the standard deviation, my eyes glaze over. People have assumed that, as a woman, I like to go shopping and to the hairdresser. The opposite is true. I don't like to do either. Shopping and going to the hairdresser are a necessary evil.

iv. Do clients want to learn?

Some clients do and others do not. The 2010 study by the Boston Consulting Group (see footnote 3) found that, generally, women are eager to learn about investments and wealth management, regardless of their level of financial knowledge. As for me, do I want to learn about standard deviation? It depends on whether I need to do so for work. But other clients, women or men, might be completely intrigued.

Watch the client. Do their eyes glaze over, or are they engaged? Women who have left financial matters to their husbands but have the ability to understand may want an advisor who is patient and willing to teach them to manage their own financial affairs. Protecting their privacy might be important to them. However, you will want to ensure you have the paper trail to prove the client understood what you were talking about. That's because her children, who may be unaware of their mother's climb up the learning curve, might be suspicious about you and looking for some reason to sue you after their mom's passing. The children may underestimate how much their mother understood and paint a picture to a judge or regulator of a vulnerable, unsophisticated old woman. If the woman had no formal education or a job that required her to understand investments, it will be the advisor's challenge to prove that they explained the investments to her in a comprehensible way. If a woman is inexperienced and unwilling to learn, ask her whether she would like to involve a relative or close friend—someone she trusts—to assist her with her investment decisions. If not, perhaps the client has a lawyer or accountant who is prepared to act as her power of attorney.

Now, the very suggestion that the client is unable to manage her own finances might be offensive. But it might also be a relief to her if you are there to help her make this transition.

You will have to navigate this issue carefully to gauge how able and willing she is to understand basic financial issues and products. If she is indeed inexperienced but able and willing to learn, it will take a lot of your time and patience. If you have neither, be honest with yourself and do not seek to service these clients. But if you do take the time, it will not be without reward, because "the women's club" is alive and kicking. Referrals will be made to those advisors who win over clients by being patient and understanding.

D. Fiduciary duty

Fiduciary duties (the duty to, among other things, put the client's interests first), and how these duties currently apply to advisors in Canada is largely misunderstood by the industry. According to common law,[26] a fiduciary relationship (the hallmarks of which are loyalty, trust, and confidence) only exists in certain circumstances. In determining whether a fiduciary duty exists, a judge will review the following five criteria:[27]

1. *Vulnerability of the client.* Is the client vulnerable, because of (for example) advanced age, or a lack of language skills, investment knowledge, education, or experience in the stock market?

2. *Trust.* Does the client repose trust and confidence in the advisor? What is the extent to which the advisor accepts that trust?

3. *Reliance.* Is there a long history of the client relying on the advisor's judgment and advice? Did the advisor represent

---

26 Applicable to all provinces in Canada except for Quebec.

27 *Hunt v. TD Securities Inc.,* 2003 Carswell Ont. 3141 at paras. 40-41, [2003] O.J. No. 3245 (Ont. C.A.).

themselves as having special skills that the client could rely on? Did the client rely on the advisor for all decisions about their account, or did the client participate in the decision-making process with the advisor?

4. *Discretion.* Does the advisor exercise discretion over the account?

5. *Professional rules of conduct.* Do the professional rules and/or code of conduct dictate that the advisor is held to a fiduciary standard?

Not all the criteria must exist; a flexible approach is applied. If either the fourth or fifth criteria applies, the advisor will likely owe the client a fiduciary duty. However, if there is no discretion exercised, or the rules of professional conduct do not dictate a fiduciary relationship, the first three criteria will be more significant in the judge's determination of whether a fiduciary relationship indeed existed.

So why am I raising fiduciary duty within the topic of women clients? Because of the growing number of elderly widows who may lack market experience. These women may be relying on their advisor. If a dispute goes to court, the judge may find such women to be more vulnerable (the first criterion). If the elderly woman client reposes her trust in the advisor and completely (blindly) relies on his advice, that points to a fiduciary relationship.

Indeed, judges might assume that women who have little market experience are in a fiduciary relationship with their advisors. But if the advisor can prove that they took the client up the learning curve and that the client understood investments and actively participated in the process, then the advisor may be able to prove to the judge that they were not in a fiduciary relationship. Why is this relevant? Because if the judge finds that there was a fiduciary relationship between the advisor and the client, and that the fiduciary duty was breached, then the advisor may not be able to rely on legislation[28] that permits the judge to apportion liability between clients and advisors. For example, 50/50 responsibility would mean the advisor is only responsible for 50% of the losses, and the client is responsible for the other 50%.

If you are servicing a client who is a novice investor and she is indeed learning about the market, either from you or someone else, and if she is engaged in decision-making, be sure to have a solid paper trail to later prove this. Without such a paper trail, you are the one who will be vulnerable.

E. Offending male clients

A bird in the hand is worth two in the bush, so if you have happy clients, and you are operating a compliant business, you will need to think long and hard about whether to change the relationship you have with clients who are couples. I am not suggesting that you cater to women to the neglect of their husbands. That may lead to the quick loss of assets under your administration. But I have been asked by advisors how to deal with the issue of servicing women clients when their husbands have prevented them from meeting.[29] Remember

---

28 For example: *Negligence Act*, RSO 1990 c.N-1 in Ontario; *Contributory Negligence Act*, RSA. 2000 c. C-27 in Alberta; *Negligence Act*, RSBC chapter 333 in British Columbia; *Contributory Negligence Act*, RS c.95 in Nova Scotia.

29 For more on this, see *Advisor at Risk*, Chapter 8.

the example of Mr. and Mrs. Bunny. Suppose Mrs. Bunny had signed a trading authorization or a power of attorney permitting Mr. Bunny to instruct the advisor on her behalf. This does not mean the advisor does not have to meet with her. Any suggestion to the contrary is dead wrong and will lead to the advisor committing regulatory and legal infractions. Assuming Mrs. Bunny is not suffering from dementia (or any illness that renders her unable to manage her own personal affairs, and there is a doctor's letter in the file to confirm this), the advisor has a regulatory and legal obligation to meet with her to ensure KYC obligations are fulfilled. The advisor needs to continue to meet with her from time to time to update her personal circumstances, including but not limited to completing a risk assessment.[30] Anything short of this exposes the advisor to regulatory and legal risk.

How does the advisor change a relationship that has been focused only on one of the two spouses (regardless of gender), to the exclusion of the other? It is difficult to suggest how to approach any particular situation. Suddenly including the wife has to be handled carefully, especially if the husband is strong-willed about not "bothering her" with these details. You will need to sell to him the importance of bringing her up to speed, for example, in case something were to happen to him.

Like with most situations, I suggest you do it slowly and make it easy for the woman to attend the meetings. For example, if the meetings with Mr. Bunny have been at your office, you could suggest changing the venue to a location more convenient to Mrs. Bunny, such as their home or near her office. You can also explain that it is a regulatory and legal obligation

---

30   See more on power of attorney in Chapter 9.

that you meet with both spouses, even though one has trading authorization for the other. You can blame it on compliance officers (or me!) who insist that you meet with his wife. As women begin to control more of the wealth, and especially knowing that a significant number of widows transfer from the advisor who serviced her deceased husband, you will be happy to have a good relationship with her after her husband passes. As offended as he might get, losing your license or risking your reputation is not worth it.

Summary

As more women are managing their own wealth, and as their share of the economy continues to expand, women clients are a major area of growth in the financial advisory industry. This is a huge opportunity that advisors can't afford to overlook. To mitigate the potential risks associated with servicing women, advisors need to address common traits but not to the exclusion of individual characteristics.

Advisors Take Action

✓ Make sure you meet with your clients' spouses. Engage and involve them in the process, and develop a relationship with them.

✓ Do not approach women clients as a homogenous group. Ask thoughtful questions to ensure you get to know each individual client.

✓ Determine the sophistication of women clients and encourage them to share private information by asking relevant questions, in a sensitive manner. Show empathy and foster trust.

✓ Be patient and willing to teach inexperienced clients, and ensure you have the paper trail to prove the client understood what you were talking about.

9

Senior Clients

S ERVICING SENIOR CLIENTS effectively is a great way to grow your business, but don't ignore the risks to both you and your elderly clients. This chapter will review both the opportunities and the risks of servicing senior clients.

It is old news that this segment of the population is growing rapidly, with expectations that it will represent between 23–25% of the total population by 2036.[1] Likely, many of your clients are already seniors, but consider the next generations as well. This sector and the generations that follow are key to an advisor's success because of the opportunities to grow the assets from your existing client base, and to help them plan for the generations that follow.

---

1   Statistics Canada, Canada Year Book 2012, available at www150.statcan.gc.ca/n1/pub/11-402-x/2011000/chap/seniors-aines/seniors-aines-eng.htm.

I. The Risks of Serving Seniors

Serving elderly clients has its challenges. Consider the following example:

Rosie is 87 years old. She is exceptionally well dressed and groomed. She has been in good health for the years that Stubby, her advisor, has been servicing her. Rosie lost her husband, Ozzy, when he was 64 years old. Rosie has been managing her financial affairs for decades, both responsibly and effectively. Stubby has recently noticed that Rosie has been missing her appointments with him. So he calls to see how she is. She sounds confused. She doesn't seem to know who is on the phone, even though she always recognized Stubby's name and voice in previous calls over the years. After a few minutes of reminders by Stubby, Rosie recognizes who she is speaking to. Due to this evidence of confusion, they decide that Rosie would visit Stubby's office the following week with her son, Luca (age 63).

When Rosie turns up with Luca, she doesn't look as she usually does. Her appearance is disheveled and unkempt. During the meeting, Rosie seems distracted when Stubby speaks. She has a faraway look in her eyes. All of this is out of character.

In a private moment, Stubby asks Luca if his mother is all right. Luca tells him not to worry. He has noticed that his mother is "losing it" and he is making arrangements for her care. Stubby tells Luca that he needs to rebalance Rosie's portfolio, but Rosie seems tired from the time they have already spent together. Luca says he will come to Stubby's office on another day to sort out the details. Luca also tells Stubby that he is impressed with him and was thinking he should open an account with Stubby, too.

Stubby realizes he completely forgot to ask Rosie or Luca if there is a valid power of attorney document signed by Rosie, appointing Luca as attorney. Stubby takes comfort from the fact that Luca attended with Rosie, and Rosie appeared comfortable sharing her personal financial information with Luca.

Stubby meets with Luca a week later so they can review Rosie's portfolio. Stubby reminds Luca of their previous review of his mother's portfolio and seeks Luca's instructions to make certain changes to her investments. Luca provides Stubby with permission to make these changes. Stubby executes the trades in accordance with Luca's instructions.

About six months later, Stubby calls Luca, again forgetting that there is no written permission from Rosie for Luca to instruct him on her behalf. The purpose of this call is to update Rosie's financial plan to incorporate plans for the next generation. Stubby wants to impress Luca, to encourage him to open an account, either before or after Rosie passes away. Luca and Stubby meet to discuss the plan, which presumably would ultimately lead to a transfer of at least some of Rosie's assets to Luca. They finalize the plan.

Two weeks later, Luca calls Stubby. He says his mother is going to move into his house immediately until a full nursing care facility is available for her. They need to pay a packer and mover and someone to arrange for the sale of her furniture. They also need money for the rent Rosie will pay Luca for the additional expenses he and his wife will incur by taking care of her. Luca says he needs the funds urgently because he cannot allow her to live on her own any longer. Deposits and payments need to be made.

Stubby arranges for funds to be transferred to a bank account Rosie provided to him just before she became ill.

Stubby doesn't know that Luca had arranged for this account to be opened between Luca and Rosie jointly. Funds are transferred to this account, with Stubby believing it is an account held by Rosie. Stubby doesn't turn his mind to how Luca would access the money from that account, and doesn't ask.

Luca tells Stubby to immediately change Rosie's address to his so that her investment statements and other mail from the dealer will be delivered to Luca's house. Stubby tells Luca that his investment dealer needs Rosie's written authorization to change the address. Luca tells Stubby to email the form to Luca so he can arrange for Rosie to sign it. The form is signed and returned to Stubby. However, Stubby has not considered whether Rosie has the mental capacity to sign the form. He does not verify the signature by comparing it to forms Rosie previously signed in Stubby's presence. The branch manager also doesn't check the form for authenticity when it is presented to her for sign-off.

Another month passes and Stubby gets another call from Luca, telling him more money is needed now for the deposit for the nursing home. Stubby has not done any research himself on nursing home costs, but information from his other clients seems to indicate the sum Luca is seeking is very high. Due to the urgency, Stubby ignores the potential red flag and arranges for funds from Rosie's account to be delivered to the bank account on file (jointly held between Luca and Rosie).

A year passes and Stubby would like to do another review of Rosie's account. It occurs to him that he needs a power of attorney document if Rosie is unable to continue to work with him and all instructions will be coming from Luca. This is discussed with Luca. Luca instead suggests that Rosie's investment account should be moved to a joint account with Luca. Stubby agrees that if the account is jointly held, he is permitted to take instructions from either one of them, and so that would indeed resolve the issue. Stubby needs Rosie's signature and Luca says that is not a problem. Again, Stubby does not consider whether Rosie has capacity to sign and he doesn't even explain the tax and other implications to Rosie of moving the account to a joint account.

The account is transferred to a joint account. Stubby and Luca continue to operate the account as a joint account, requiring only Luca's instructions. Another year goes by, with withdrawals being made for Rosie's care, and to help Luca with a downpayment on a larger home. Apparently, Rosie isn't happy in the nursing home, so she spends about half of her time staying with Luca and his wife in their home, hence the need for Luca to buy a larger home.

Stubby is becoming concerned, because Rosie's account is being managed conservatively and is not making much in the way of returns. With the recent spending, there has been a significant decrease in Rosie's money. Stubby expresses this concern to Luca, who has a solution. Luca tells Stubby that his account with his other advisor is making much greater returns than his mother's. He suggests that Stubby emulate the investments in Luca's account. Stubby, a bit offended, reviews Luca's account statement and tells him the investments in his account are far more aggressive and risky than would be suitable for Rosie. Luca says that because he is the sole beneficiary of Rosie's account, which is now a joint account, he is in a position to request that Stubby invest more aggressively. Stubby, feeling uncomfortable but not wanting to lose the business, shifts Rosie's investments into more aggressive ones, albeit not as aggressive as Luca's suggestions. Luca periodically calls Stubby to arrange for withdrawals to take care of his mother. Stubby expresses concern that Rosie may run out of money if

Luca continues to withdraw at this rate. Luca is offended. He says that he is very responsible and takes good care of Rosie and will do so for the rest of her life. That same day, unbeknownst to Stubby, Luca signs documents with a new advisor to transfer the joint account assets to another dealer. Stubby notices and doesn't know what to do. He is worried that maybe Luca is up to no good. He says nothing to his supervisor or compliance. He thinks it is better to keep quiet at this point.

The story of Rosie, Stubby, and Luca is a composite of several cases I have encountered in my practice. Only the names and some minor facts have been changed. While I cannot tell you exactly what happened, suffice it to say that Stubby does not come out of this unscathed. Rosie did indeed suffer from dementia. Luca had no authority whatsoever to manage his mother's affairs and withdraw money from her account. As it turned out, he was not the sole beneficiary of his mother's estate. When Stubby found himself before the judge, he was in deep trouble. Further, when the securities dealer read the claim, setting out the facts as described above, and confronted Stubby, who could not deny these facts, Stubby's securities dealer terminated him and filed a termination notice with his regulator that would make it extremely difficult for Stubby to be registered with another dealer.

If you think this is an unlikely set of events, think again. Let's unpack all the issues in this case study, to ensure something like this never happens to you. Because you, like Stubby, would not likely get out unscathed.

A. Privacy

There is no question that Stubby breached Rosie's privacy rights. Stubby called Rosie's son without her authorization. Stubby even shared with Luca the sum of the assets and the investment details without Rosie's authorization. Without written authorization from Rosie, Luca is not entitled to any of this information. That authorization could be in the form of a power of attorney or a simple handwritten letter, as long as any authorization given was signed while Rosie had the capacity to do so.

B. Capacity/incapacity

Somehow, regulators have made identifying incapacity or dementia the advisor's and dealer's problem. Regulators want advisors and dealers to ensure they are not taking instructions from clients who do not have the capacity to understand the decisions being made about their personal property. Regulators also want advisors and dealers to protect clients from abuses and fraud. This is the case even if the ones committing the fraud have the authority to instruct the advisor through a power of attorney document or otherwise, like a close relative.

Unless the client has capacity, you cannot take instructions from them. So it is crucial for advisors to be satisfied that the client has the capacity to give instructions on a trade or otherwise. This is the basis of many estate challenges: whether or not the client had capacity on the date that they signed any documents. Those documents could be internal to the dealer (KYC, LTA, etc.) or external, such as a power of attorney document. The client's medical records may be examined to determine whether there were capacity issues on the date of the document or of the trade. This is truly a problem for advisors.

And the problem is exacerbated by the fact that advisors are not qualified to determine whether a client has capacity or not. Even if the advisor suspects that the client is not as sharp as they once were, this does not mean they do not have capacity. Often, the onset of dementia is gradual. Advisors and dealers have the challenge of determining the point at which the client becomes incapacitated.[2] For some time before the onset of dementia, Rosie may have suffered memory loss, but she still may have had the capacity to manage her financial affairs. The number of people over 60 years old affected by dementia is astounding. Research shows that one in nine people aged 65 and older (11%) have Alzheimer's disease. More disconcerting is that more than one-third of people aged 85 and older (32%) have Alzheimer's disease.[3]

Here are some telltale signs:[4]

- The investor appears unable to comprehend simple concepts (in contrast to previously being able to grasp more complex concepts).

- The investor appears to have memory loss, especially in contrast to previous experiences with the client.

- The investor appears to have difficulty speaking or communicating.

---

2   "Canada's investment industry: Protecting senior investors—compliance, supervisor and other practices when serving senior investors," The Investment Industry Association of Canada (IIAC), March 18, 2014, page 5.

3   These are US statistics: see "2016 Alzheimer's disease facts and figures," Alzheimer's Association, page 17; however, Canadians figures reported by Statistics Canada and published in the article "Health reports: Alzheimer's disease and other dementias in Canada," by Suzy L. Wong, Heather Gilmour, and Pamela L. Ramage-Morin, May 18, 2016, are similar (see www.statca.gc.ca/pub/82-003-x/2016005/article/14613-eng.htm).

4   IIAC, "Canada's investment industry," page 12.

- The investor makes decisions that are inconsistent with their previous long-term goals or commitments.

- The investor refuses to follow appropriate investment advice; this may be of particular concern when the advice is consistent with previously stated investment objectives.

- The investor appears to be concerned that there might be funds missing from their account, even though reviews of the account indicate there were no unauthorized money movements or no money movement at all.

- The investor is not aware of, or does not understand, recently completed financial transactions.

- The investor appears to be disoriented with surroundings or social settings.

- The investor appears uncharacteristically unkempt or forgetful.

- The investor's recurring cognitive problems become worse over time.

- The investor displays behavior that is out of character (e.g., the frugal client who becomes a spendthrift; the client who wants to upset a long-established investment strategy).

- The investor has difficulty understanding important aspects of the account (particularly if they had understood these issues previously).

Advisors need to be sensitive to changes in client behavior. However, some clients are very good at masking their inability to understand. This can make it difficult to detect any cognitive issues, especially early on in the onset of dementia.

The more senior clients you have, the more clients you will have with capacity issues. With the average age of the population increasing, the advisor needs to be on the lookout for signs so that discussions can be had with the client before it is too late.

Once the client is incapacitated, the advisor cannot seek or obtain instructions from the client or ask them to sign documents. If you have not had discussions with your client before they become incapacitated, you will have to seek direction from compliance. You could arrange a meeting with the client, preferably with a family member as well. You need to handle this carefully so as not to breach privacy laws. Alternatively, you can contact the Office of the Public Guardian and Trustee.

You can see how important it is, as part of the Know Your Client exercise, to know in advance where the client's power of attorney (POA) document is kept and, even better, who the person or people are who have been chosen as the attorney for the client's personal property. You can then contact the person (or lawyer or the attorney themselves) to obtain the POA. You can then take instructions from the attorney appointed by the client without breaching privacy laws.

C. Power of attorney

Here are some of the most important issues arising from power of attorney documents:

i. *Making assumptions*

Without a document that directs the advisor to follow instructions from someone other than the client, the advisor cannot act. The advisor needs to see the POA document. Advisors cannot assume, like in the scenario with Rosie and Stubby, that the one child the advisor is aware of is indeed the only one who would or could have authorization. It could be that Rosie didn't trust her son and arranged for a friend or another relative to be her attorney for personal property. Don't assume anything, and don't take instructions from anyone without having such a document.

In the example of Stubby, this advisor was acting in a completely unauthorized manner. There was no POA. If indeed Rosie was incapacitated at the time Stubby reached out to Luca, it may have been too late for her to sign a power of attorney. She may not have had the mental capacity to understand the implications of the document and the authority she was granting to Luca over her personal property.

Accordingly, it is imperative that you ensure every client has signed a power of attorney document and that you know where it is kept. If your dealer has its own document, which most do not, you will want to obtain direction from the dealer about whether you should ask the client to sign the dealer's document, or if it is enough to rely on the client's own power of attorney.

ii. *Not asking about a power of attorney document*

In the scenario, Stubby didn't even ask Rosie or Luca for the POA document. Instead, Stubby proceeded as if Luca had the authority to manage his mother's assets. After the assets were placed into a joint account, there was no need for a POA because Luca had ownership of the assets as joint account holder. However, since Stubby should not have placed the assets into a joint account without instructions from Rosie herself, he exposed himself to liability for that specific action, as well as for anything that happened to Rosie's investments thereafter.

Stubby should have asked for the POA at the outset. He should have scrutinized it to ensure it was authentic and enforceable. You need to be careful when presented with a power of attorney document to read it carefully and ensure you clearly understand the authority and any limits on it, as set out in the document.

iii. *The trigger*

The POA can be a standard document, or one that contains clauses to reflect what the client wants. It can be that the attorney for personal property is authorized to give directions on the client's accounts immediately upon the POA being signed, or only after the client has become incapacitated. The POA could be effective with or without an official declaration of incapacity. It could be triggered by various methods, depending on what the client wanted at the time they effected it. For example, the POA might require that a doctor confirm incapacity. Or it might require that a capacity expert run the client through a battery of tests and prepare an official report. It could be that the POA is triggered not by incapacity at all but by a declaration in writing by the client that they want the power of attorney document to be triggered.

Because the power of attorney document can vary, you need to read it carefully and send a copy to compliance to ensure you can begin to take instructions from the attorney.[5]

---

5   The terms 'attorney' and 'grantee' are interchangeable. I will refer only to attorney throughout this chapter when referring to the person granted authority.

iv. Authority and its limits

The power of attorney document could limit the extent of authority of the person chosen. Alternatively, it could be very broad. Limits may be that the attorney can trade on the account but cannot redeem funds. It could be that trades and redemptions are permitted by the attorney but the authority does not extend to withdrawals. It is important to find out from your compliance/legal team whether the authority is limited in any manner so that you do not permit the attorney for property to direct you beyond what is permitted and intended by the client.

v. Client's best interests

The advisor and dealer need to always consider instructions provided to ensure all activities in the account are in the client's best interest. That was not the case with Rosie. That means the advisor can refuse to follow the instructions from the attorney for property. A common example of this is when the attorney instructs the advisor to change the risk profile for the account to allow for riskier investments. It is very unlikely you would be able to produce evidence that would satisfy a judge or a regulator that such a change is in the client's best interest. You would have to refuse any such instructions. For redemptions and withdrawals from the account that seem excessive for the client's needs, you need to satisfy yourself and your dealer that such redemptions and payments are in the client's best interest.

Suppose that Rosie's account was not jointly held with her son but instead was in her name only. The advisor, Stubby, was being asked to send checks for sums that seemed to be excessive for payment of Rosie's support. Assuming further that Luca was operating under a power of attorney, inquiries should have been made and perhaps the money requested should have been refused.

There are circumstances in which the attorney admits that withdrawals are for their own benefit or the benefit of someone other than the client. The advisor and dealer must refuse to carry out such instructions.

Be cautious and always ensure all instructions are consistent with your client's needs and values and not the needs and values of the person appointed under the power of attorney document. Seeking legal advice before problems arise is significantly less expensive than the cost of litigation or regulatory defense against charges of unsuitable/unauthorized trading that can arise from complaints of other beneficiaries.

vi. Client signature

The POA document has to be signed while the client has the capacity to do so. Be suspicious if you receive a POA document signed and dated after you know the client was already incapacitated. Look at the witness to the client's signature and determine if it is the attorney who witnessed the document. If it is, that is not permitted.[6]

Clearly, the POA document is not straightforward. It needs to be carefully scrutinized to ensure it is authentic and to understand the extent of, or limits to, the authorization given to the advisor to follow the instructions of the attorney.

---

6   *Substitute Decisions Act*, 1992, SO 1992, c. 30, s. 10 (2).

vii. *Contact with the client*

Just because the advisor is taking instructions from someone other than the client (whether it is pursuant to a power of attorney document or a limited trading authorization), the advisor should not cut themselves off from the ultimate client. The client may be choosing to have someone else manage their affairs without having any signs of incapacity for other reasons. In these circumstances, you need to remain in contact with the client. Further, if someone you have never heard of presents themselves to you without any warning from the client, you should pick up the phone and attempt to contact the client. Obtain confirmation from the client that you can and should take instructions from the stranger. Make sure this is not senior abuse or fraud (to be discussed in the next section). Once you are satisfied, continue to keep in touch with the client, particularly if there are questionable transactions requested that do not seem to be in the client's best interest.

What if the client doesn't have a POA document? If a client doesn't have a power of attorney signed before they become incapacitated, then court proceedings need to take place so that an application can be made to the court to appoint a guardian of property. If there is no one who will make that application, then the advisor, through their dealer, needs to inform the provincial office of the public guardian and trustee.[7]

D. Suitability

About 90% of my litigation cases are those in which seniors are suing for alleged losses associated with unsuitable investments.

---

7   These may have different names in different provinces. In Ontario, it is called the Office of the Public Guardian and Trustee.

IIROC, MFDA, and OBSI report that a significant proportion of their proceedings involve the issue of suitability, and they have also expressed the need for and include on their websites materials to assist senior investors. Combining the two, the issue of suitability and seniors, has its unique features.

i. Capital preservation

The challenge with suitability for seniors is that, with very few exceptions, these are not years in which people can easily replenish their accumulated capital. If there is a severe market correction, the senior's exposure is, arguably, more significant. As well, many seniors have not saved enough for retirement, given how long people are living, and will run out of money before they pass away. That creates a serious dilemma for advisors. They are forced, on the one hand, to keep their senior clients in safe investments so they don't lose money if there is a market correction. On the other hand, seniors may be worried that the safe investments will not yield the returns necessary.[8]

It is crucial to have a fresh look at your client's circumstances to reassess their risk profile—first, as the client nears retirement, and then again at retirement. Ensure you get this right! What you do not want is to get the risk profile wrong and have the client panic when they lose money due to a market correction. Panic leads clients to make bad decisions, including selling at the bottom of the market and losing even more money by spending it on lawyers in order to sue their advisors.

---

8   See 'risk need' in Chapter 6. Clients need to be reassessed at this time in their lives to ensure the advisor gets it right!

ii. Time horizon

A potentially shorter time horizon[9] renders the elderly more vulnerable to market fluctuations. If elderly clients suffer a market decline shortly after they stop working and need to make redemptions for withdrawals when the portfolio is down, they would be doing so at the worst possible time. If the recently retired senior gets nervous after a market decline and instructs their advisor to sell, the losses suffered will be at the beginning of their retirement. This will replace the value of their portfolio, which is worse than making this decision after decades of investment growth.[10]

You need to consider when and how much liquidity your client needs to retire. If the client is already retired, determine how much they can afford to spend each year without running out of money.

Even if the client is flush, make sure there is sufficient liquidity so that the client can meet spending needs and obligations for the duration of the market downturn, as well as the liquidity necessary for a rainy day.

iii. Overemphasis on 'risk need'

The concept of 'risk need', discussed in Chapter 6, has become an important factor when choosing investments for seniors who are worried that they have not saved enough for their retirement. Those same seniors, or their estates, quickly turn

---

9   I say potentially because seniors have been identified as 60 and over and may live past 90; 30 years is not a short time horizon, but one never knows how long the senior will live.

10   Tara Siegel Bernard, "An adage adjustment for investors at retirement," New York Times, September 14, 2013.

against advisors if the risk need factor has led to riskier investments resulting in losses that they could not afford. Regulators and SROs have been clear that risk need cannot be the driver of whether or not an investment is suitable.[11] My response to advisors facing this dilemma is that the seniors got themselves into this situation, either because they didn't plan far enough in advance, quit working too early, didn't save enough, or spent too much. Many elderly clients in this situation seek to move from their old advisor to a new one, hoping for better returns. Here are a few strong messages for those new advisors about these types of clients:

1. The previous investment risk was too high. If the client was in higher-risk investments, it could be that the client pushed the previous advisor to buy higher-risk securities on which the client lost money. Be careful as this client can turn on you just like they turned on the previous advisor.

2. The client spent too much. If the client is in worse condition than before and has not saved enough for retirement, don't make this your problem. This client is in trouble by their own making and you may not be able to help them. If these are new clients, you may want to rethink whether you even want to open an account for people who have not saved enough for retirement and want the advisor to bail them out. Instead of caving in to pressure from these clients, build a plan with them so that they realize they must change their behavior. If they are unable to change, they may come back to haunt you. Put everything in writing so

---

11   See Chapter 6, footnote 3 (page 120) and footnote 7 (page 133).

that later you will have a paper trail to prove that you fulfilled your duty to the client.

3. Unexpected expenses. These can have many causes. For example, certain costly drugs and medical procedures are not covered by either health insurance or government plans. Another expense seniors may not have planned for is supporting grown children or grandchildren through hardships like divorce, medical expenses, or care for grandchildren. Some people cannot say no, which can leave them vulnerable financially. They may then turn to their advisor for a solution. In situations like this, advisors may have to refuse the client's request for investments that have the potential for higher returns but come with more risk that the client can bear.

4. Regulatory presumptions. What will happen if these clients who had a need for capital and who insisted that their advisor put them in higher-risk investments sue or complain to the regulator? Regulators have certain presumptions. For example, regulators have expressed that there is an assumption that all senior clients should be in low-risk investments, unless there is strong evidence to the contrary. However, there are many sophisticated seniors who have run their own businesses, own properties, and are actively engaged in their investment choices who insist on high-risk investments. While higher risk might be suitable for these clients, do not kid yourself: these are the same clients who will turn on you if the market doesn't co-operate. The advisor and dealer will have to prove that the client was sophisticated and understood the risk of the trades.

iv. Death of a spouse

The death of a spouse can impact the suitability of investments, especially if the spouse who passed was the one who took a more active role in the management of the family finances. The advisor might have to take a more active role to bring the client up the learning curve, or adjust the risk profile to reflect the client's inability to understand more complex investments. Remember, if the client does not understand an investment, it is best not to have them investing in it.[12]

v. Suitability on joint accounts

Can an advisor compromise on what is suitable for a client? Consider two people who are joint owners of an account and have different risk profiles. Can the advisor suggest a compromise to satisfy both people? No, the joint account cannot be a compromise. If two people want a joint account but their risk profile for that account is not aligned, then they need two separate accounts instead. Due to the difference in suitability, it is inappropriate to push the risk on the account higher or lower to satisfy one client over the other.

vi. Suitability and beneficiaries/POA

A common scenario that I have witnessed is when there isn't a joint account but the attorney wants the risk profile raised because they expect to be the beneficiary of the estate and want the risk profile to be more aligned with their own. This is wrong. If the advisor succumbs to such pressure for fear of losing the account, they may later be subject to regulatory scrutiny, with all of the public exposure and penalties that go along with it, if a complaint is made.

---

12   See Chapter 5 of this book, as well as *Advisor at Risk*, Chapter 5.

If an advisor buys unsuitable investments for a senior and the client passes away, the other beneficiaries might well scrutinize the investment account. If money was lost due to higher risk, the other beneficiaries may go after you rather than the attorney who instructed you on the trades.

Always remember who your client is, regardless of who you receive instructions from. You need to protect your elderly clients and cannot give in to pressure from attorneys who believe the money is theirs even though the senior is still alive and continues to need money to support themselves.

E. Joint accounts

Joint accounts are too often recommended as a way to avoid payment of probate taxes, a tax imposed on estate assets after the death of the client. The concept is that the assets will flow to the joint account holder after the other person dies and so will not form part of the estate. However, the advisor needs to explain to the client all the possible implications associated with making an account joint, so that the client can make an informed decision. Here are a few of those implications:

1. *Tax implications.* If there is a movement of ownership from sole to joint, for tax purposes, there will be a deemed disposition of the account at the time of transfer to joint, which may trigger tax obligations. Therefore, even though the estate can avoid the probate tax if the assets are held jointly, the former sole account holder could be hit with a big tax bill during their lifetime. Take the case of Rosie, her greedy son, and her hapless advisor. In the year that the account is changed to be held jointly with Luca, Rosie will be taxed on all capital gains as if she made a disposition, even if the assets are not redeemed. However, it will not be until

after Rosie passes away that her last will and testament will reveal the beneficiaries of her estate. If most of her assets are in her jointly held investment account (with Luca) and there is nothing in the estate for the other beneficiaries, there might be challenges in court about whether the assets in the joint account should be part of the estate, and therefore divided among all the beneficiaries. If the other beneficiaries prove that Rosie did not intend to give Luca the money but instead it was transferred to be held jointly for convenience, the assets will be deemed to be part of the estate and the probate tax will apply. Rosie needs to know all of this before any transfer to a joint account with Luca.

2. *Removal of funds.* If the account is jointly held, then both holders legally own 100% of the account and can withdraw it entirely without any notification to the other person. Rosie risks the account being emptied by Luca, without notice to her.

3. *Creditors.* Since joint account holders both own the entire account, the assets are subject to collection by creditors. In the case of Rosie and Luca, if Luca owes any money—to a bank or credit card company, for example—the account assets can be seized by his creditors.

4. *Spouses.* If Luca is married and he and his wife separate, the assets in the joint account are part of the family assets, so Luca's wife may have a right to a portion of the assets in the account.

Seniors must understand each of these risks before signing any documents changing the ownership of the account to joint. There may be very little benefit to the senior in doing so, and a significant amount of risk. If the senior wants to do tax planning, they should retain tax lawyers and accountants rather than seek to simply move assets to a joint account. Advisors need to alert their elderly clients of the risks, and ensure any tax advice comes from someone qualified to give it.

II. Senior Abuse and the "F-words": Fiduciary Duty and Fraud

The two "F-words" mean that there is a special degree of care and attention needed when working with senior clients.

A. Fiduciary duty and communication with seniors and/or POA

As I outlined in Chapter 8, in all common law provinces, there are five criteria to determine whether an advisor[13] owes a fiduciary duty to a client. Two of those five criteria that apply to the elderly, in particular, are vulnerability and reliance.

---

13 Portfolio managers, due to the nature of the discretionary trading, have a fiduciary duty. See: *Kent v. May*, 2001 CarswellAlta 721, 298 A.R. 71 (Alta. QB) at para. 51, aff'd (2002), 317 A.R. 381 (Alta. CA); TD Waterhouse Canada Inc. et al., Re, 32 OSCB 5675 (OSC) at para 35; *Hodgkinson v. Simms*, 1994 Carswell BC 438, 5 ETR (2d) 1 (SCC) at para 44; and Code of Ethics and standards of Professional Conduct, CFA Institute, s. III(A): "Loyalty, Prudence, and Care. Members and Candidates have a duty of loyalty to their clients and must act with reasonable care and exercise prudent judgment. Members and Candidates must act for the benefit of their clients and place their clients' interests before their employer's or their own interests."

Judges and arbitrators tend to presume that there is a fiduciary relationship between an elderly client and their advisor on the basis that elderly clients likely rely heavily on their advisors and trust them implicitly. The advisor may have the evidence to prove otherwise.

B. Identify fraud through communication with elderly clients

Protecting seniors from fraud is easier said than done. Yet regulators have sent a clear message to advisors that they are counting on them to be the first line of defense against fraudsters. That's because, presumably, advisors have regular contact with their clients and know them sufficiently well to recognize something out of the ordinary—a possible sign that a fraudster is at work.

Fraud against the elderly seems to happen more frequently than you might expect. From my experience, these fraudsters fall into one of two categories: 1) someone the client has known for years and trusts, such as a family member, close friend, or a trusted professional such as an accountant, lawyer, or previously licensed advisor (someone who, unbeknownst to the senior, has lost their license); or 2) a stranger who seems to appear out of nowhere, seeking to "help" your senior client, while actually helping themselves to the senior's assets. Let's look at each category.

i. Someone the client knows and trusts

Elderly clients can become vulnerable to abuse by family members, friends, and trusted advisors. Seniors may only have one person willing to take care of them, say, bringing them meals and helping with everyday needs. A sense of dependence may arise. If someone wants to take advantage of the senior, that person is in a prime position to do so.

There are also close family friends and advisors who have had a longstanding relationship with the entire family and have earned their trust over time. The elderly client often trusts these professionals like they would a family member or close friend. As well, family members or friends might have access to all the elderly person's banking information and other assets, and may take an active role by giving instructions to bankers and advisors.

In the example of Rosie and Luca, the advisor trusted that Luca was acting in Rosie's best interest but the advisor may have been blinded by his desire not to lose the assets to another advisor. This should never be a motivating force.

Rosie's advisor, Stubby, did not ensure that proper steps were taken to protect his elderly client by obtaining a power of attorney document and ensuring that Rosie, when she was of sound mind, chose Luca to act on her behalf. It could be that Rosie gave power of attorney to someone else. Stubby made no inquiries. Instead, he assumed Rosie trusted Luca because when she was already losing capacity, it was Luca who attended the meetings and seemed to be stepping up to care for his mother. If Stubby had discussions with Rosie before she showed signs of dementia, he might have discovered who she trusted and where he could locate her POA document. By the time she showed signs of dementia, it may have been too late.

Always keep an elderly client's goals and needs distinct from those of the family or friend, even if they also are clients. This is especially true when you are led to believe that the person acting on the senior's behalf is the only beneficiary. There is no way to be certain of this until after the last will and testament is read. If the assets have not been managed properly, the other beneficiaries can and will bring proceedings.

Don't assume the person who has power of attorney is honest and acting to care for and protect the elderly client. There are enough examples in my practice alone to confirm this can be untrue. Regulators have turned to advisors to be on high alert for potential mismanagement, so advisors have no choice but to scrutinize the instructions received to ensure they are in the best interest of the elderly client.

ii. Strangers

Fraudsters, through obituaries and other sources, identify widows and widowers who are particularly vulnerable and move in on them. These strangers can be professional manipulators, gaining the confidence of these vulnerable seniors quickly. It has happened that seniors have called their advisors seeking large redemptions, or transactions that are out of character. This could be a red flag for the advisor.

The senior might have what seem to be legitimate explanations for the first few redemptions: funeral expenses for a spouse, the cost of fixing up the house for sale, a trip to visit a family member. There is no shortage of good reasons for redemptions and withdrawals after the death of a spouse. However, the better you know your client and communicate with them regularly, regardless of whether there is a POA in place, the more sensitive you will be to whether the amount of the redemption, and the reason for it, make sense. For example, if the widower says the reason for a $20,000 redemption is to visit his sister in South Africa and you know he doesn't have a sister, then that will most certainly be suspicious. It could be a sign of dementia, or it could be that a fraudster is behind the scenes. Either way, you need to be concerned for the well-being of the client.

C. What do you do if you suspect fraud?

Regardless of whether the fraudster is a family/friend/professional or a stranger, advisors have to be on the alert for redemptions. Here are a few things to consider and to do when you suspect something is amiss:

1. Note that while it is the client's money and they have the right to withdraw it on very short notice, large, small, and frequent redemptions can place the senior in peril.

2. Never trust the person in charge just because they have a power of attorney; always be suspicious.

3. Look for signs of incapacity in every visit or discussion with the elderly client.

4. Examine the reason and the amount of the redemption to determine the reasonableness.

5. If the senior is providing reasons for the redemptions, inquire further to test if these are canned answers being fed to the client by someone behind the scenes.

6. If a stranger appears with the client, do a search on the internet to see if there is any public information about the person that might confirm your suspicion.

7. If there are suspicious circumstances, escalate these to compliance or legal and follow the internal protocols set out in your dealer's processes and procedures manual.

8. Educate your elderly clients about common fraudulent activities, such as people trying to get information from them over the telephone or internet, or disguising themselves as bankers or dealers.

9. Beware of email hacking. Be sure that all emailed instructions are confirmed by telephone. Otherwise, this is a breach of regulations.

Always try to protect your senior clients. You are the first line of defense and will be sued if there is a fraud. Remember, once redeemed and the money is gone, the advisor and dealer will be seen as the ones with deep pockets.

Summary

Seniors are a rapidly growing segment of the population. Servicing senior clients effectively is a great way for advisors to grow their business, but advisors need to be alert to the risks to both themselves and their elderly clients.

Advisors Take Action

✓ Make sure that elderly clients have the capacity to give instructions. Be on the lookout for signs of incapacity and be sensitized to changes in your clients' behavior.

✓ Find out where your client's power of attorney document is kept and who has been chosen as the attorney for the client's personal property. Don't take instructions from anyone without having such a document.

✓ Read power of attorney documents carefully in order to understand the authority and any limits. Send a copy to your compliance team to confirm that you can take instructions from the attorney.

✓ Always remember who your client is, regardless of whom you receive instructions from. Refuse to carry out any instructions that are not in your client's interest.

✓ As your clients near retirement, take a fresh look at their circumstances to reassess their risk profile and capacity. Repeat this again at retirement.

✓ Alert your elderly clients to the risks of changing to a joint account. Ensure any tax advice comes from someone qualified to give it.

10

Preparing for the Complaint

T HE MAIN PURPOSE of this chapter is to prepare you for
what could lie ahead if you do not ensure communication
is clear and properly documented.[1] The secondary purpose is to prepare you so that if a complaint, regulatory probe,
or litigation does occur, you are equipped with the necessary
information to not make the same mistakes that others have
made, thereby making matters worse for yourself.

I. Receiving the Complaint

When there is a demand for reimbursement from the dealer/
advisor, the client complaint usually begins with a telephone
call or a complaint letter.

---

1   For a full discussion of litigation and regulatory process, see *Advisor at Risk,* Chapters
    11 and 12.

A. Telephone call

If the complaint comes in as a telephone call, ask the client to put their complaint in writing. Then report it immediately to compliance, whether the client puts it in writing or not. While you are on the phone, be careful. Do not do any of the things that many advisors tend to do—things that make matters *much* worse. Take this "war story," for example:

MRS. KOO: Hello, this is Mrs. Koo, again.

ADVISOR: Hello Mrs. Koo, how are you today?

MRS. KOO: Well. I am upset because I just looked at my statement and I think I lost money, again. You know, I cannot afford to lose any more money. This is the third statement in a row where my investments have been going down, not up. I am worried. I think these investments have not been right for me. What do I do? How can I get this money back?

ADVISOR: I am really sorry, Mrs. Koo, but the market is just not co-operating. You have made money in the past. Sometimes the market goes up and sometimes it goes down. You need to take the good with the bad. Don't worry, I will take care of you. Be patient.

MRS. KOO: I am serious. These investments are not right for me. I can't continue to lose money.

SO, WHAT DID the advisor say that was the wrong thing to say? Quite a few things, in fact. Here is list of telephone dos and don'ts:

1. ***Do not apologize.*** Some advisors tend to apologize, either because they are feeling sorry about the losses, or they want to appease the client. Either way, this can spur a

client to action through a complaint or court proceeding. Don't do it.

2. ***Do not ignore the client.*** This client is upset and is complaining.[2] This advisor has likely not managed the client's expectations and/or assessed her risk profile properly. If the advisor had done so, the client should not be surprised by her account fluctuations. The advisor needs to take notes of what the client says and report it up the ranks to the branch manager and compliance officer. The advisor should not wait until the client sends something in writing to report it.

3. ***Do not suggest you will reimburse the client.*** When the advisor says that he will take care of the client, this statement could be interpreted as an admission of liability or promise of reimbursement for losses. The advisor is not permitted to settle matters directly with clients. Offering to pay the client directly for her losses without the involvement of the dealer could be viewed as both an admission of wrongdoing and an infraction.

With the ease with which telephone calls, and all conversations, can be taped, the advisor should not be surprised if the client has taped the conversation. So even more vigilance about what you say is key.

So what should the advisor do and say during such a call?

---

2   SROs have defined 'complaint' broadly to include verbal complaints, so these need to be reported to the branch manager and compliance. See MFDA Policy 3 and IIROC Rule 3100.

1. *Say very little and take notes.* The key is to say as little as possible. Just collect information from the client and take very detailed notes.

2. *Keep emotions in check.* Try to keep your feelings and reactions under control during the call, and get off the telephone as quickly as possible, without being either (to the one extreme) apologetic or (to the other extreme) defensive, rude or aggressive.

3. *Take time to consider.* Tell the client that you have taken notes and want to reflect on the matter, and say that you will get right back to them. If the client inquires, emphasize that you need at least 24 hours to consider what should be done.

4. *Report it up the ranks.* Even if the client says they will not issue a complaint because they don't want to get the advisor in trouble, you are still required to communicate this in writing to your branch manager and to compliance. I have seen advisors brush the call under the rug, and it comes back to haunt them. A complaining client will likely pursue the complaint at a later date. The fact that the client previously expressed their dissatisfaction in a call to the advisor will definitely come to light. If that happens, the advisor will be accused of failing to report a client complaint, which, if true, would be a separate infraction. All directions by your branch manager or compliance should be confirmed in an email. For example, if you are directed to call the client back to discuss selling the investments at a loss and choosing less risky alternatives, then set that out in an email to the compliance

officer and continue to take notes, as well as document and communicate with your branch manager and compliance.[3]

B. Complaint/demand letter

The purpose of the complaint letter is to express, in clear language, what the complaint is about, and what remedy the complainant is seeking. So, Mrs. Koo, in our example, is complaining that the investments were unsuitable because they were too risky, and is seeking payment of money to reflect losses.

The complaint letter is sometimes written by the client, a relative of the client, a new advisor to whom the client intends to move their money, or a lawyer. Even if it is written by someone other than the client, it could be signed by the client.

The letter could be addressed to the dealer, insurance company, or managing general agent (MGA) and copied to the regulator. It may or may not be addressed to the advisor or their supervisor.

Here is what a properly written letter would look like:

Dear Sirs/Mesdames:

I have been retained by Mrs. Shmoo Koo, widow of Mr. Koo, with no experience in investing. Mrs. Koo has been a client of yours for two years, having moved her money from the bank, where she invested only in GICs. The $750,000 she invested with you was the proceeds of Mr. Koo's life insurance and her

---

3   I do not think it is a good idea for the advisor to have any involvement with attempts to resolve the complaints; it puts the advisor into a conflict with the client and, because the matter is emotionally charged for both advisor and client, the resolution should be handled by someone removed from the situation, like the branch manager or compliance officer.

total inheritance. Mr. Koo wanted to make sure his wife was well taken care of and bought an insurance policy that would enable her to live on these proceeds for the rest of her life.

In the past two years, Mrs. Koo has complained about the substantial losses in her account and her recent account statement indicates that the balance is now $554,723. Mrs. Koo gave you this money to invest to increase it, not lose it. Now she is losing sleep worrying that she will run out of money.

We hereby demand reimbursement of her losses, plus a return equal to what a $750,000 portfolio of GICs would have yielded in the past two years, otherwise we will pursue all remedies against you, which could include a complaint to your regulator, a complaint to the OBSI, or court proceedings. If this is necessary, we will be seeking reimbursement of all legal fees.

Govern yourselves accordingly as you will receive no further notice.

(Sincerely, etc.)

If the letter is addressed only to the advisor, it must be reported to the branch manager and the dealer's compliance department. The dealer, in turn, might be obliged to report the complaint to the regulator, which often triggers a parallel regulatory investigation.[4]

I have also seen the complaint delivered only to the regulator. This can be a problem because often the regulator investigates and refuses to provide a copy of the letter to the advisor and dealer. This sometimes results in the contents of the letter being a mystery throughout the regulator's investigation.

---

4   The investigating regulator could be an SRO (IIROC or MFDA), the provincial insurance regulators, or any of the securities commissions.

If the advisor and/or dealer has errors and omissions insurance, they should put their brokers on notice.

i. Quality of the complaint letter

The complaint (or demand) letter usually overstates the facts and the sum that the client has actually lost. As far as I am concerned, an overstated demand letter is least effective because a basic investigation will immediately reveal the flaws. These flaws will hinder an early and reasonable settlement.

I once received a letter from a lawyer who must have thought the fact that the client was in his 80s was his strongest argument. So he began the letter like this: "I have been retained by Mr. Jones [not his real name], an 81-year-old senior citizen."

I didn't find the first sentence persuasive, as it was redundant that an 81-year-old is a senior citizen. As I reviewed the file and found little or no obvious exposure for the advisor, I felt the letter confirmed that indeed the strongest fact Mr. Jones had was his advanced years. I wrote a strong letter, with tons of meat on the bones, explaining why the client had no case beyond a superficial statement about his age, because he was a sophisticated client with many years of investment experience in highly risky investments.

While overstating is a mistake, sometimes I receive demand letters that are well done and have details and supporting documents for a strong case. However, even these letters need a deep-dive exploration into the facts, because the allegations, although worrisome, may not be true.

The more details in the demand letter, the better it is for the dealer and advisor, as they will know what the issues are. They can explore the issues thoroughly instead of trying to guess what the client complaint is about. Such clear letters may be the difference between an early settlement or not.

ii. *Complaint letter don'ts*

Here is what an advisor should not do after they receive a complaint letter:

1. The advisor should not shred the letter and hope that the complaint will go away.
2. The advisor should not call the complainant to try to either talk them into withdrawing the complaint or resolve it with a private payment that is off the dealer's books.
3. The advisor should not send emails to the client in response to the complaint.

Human nature is such that advisors sometimes act emotionally and make bad decisions that get them into more trouble. Any one of these steps would be a regulatory infraction.

II. What to Do with the Complaint?

So what are the first things you should do if a complaint letter arrives?

A. Breathe

This is likely one of the most stressful experiences for licensed professionals. In a split second you realize that your reputation, license, and money are at risk. Before you do anything irrational, breathe, and try to collect yourself. Don't begin an email-writing or calling-everyone-you-know tirade. You could do more damage to yourself by doing something rash. The most important piece of advice I can give you is this: DO NOT CALL THE CLIENT; DO NOT CORRESPOND WITH THE CLIENT IN ANY MANNER WHATSOEVER.

Because advisors are naturally emotionally involved, they may be unable to approach the matter objectively to assess the merits of the complaint. That is one of the reasons why advisors are not permitted to try to settle the matter with the client, unless there are clear, written directions from the branch manager or compliance. Instead, they must rely on the dealer and its compliance team to assess the complaint and decide how to respond. Further, the dealer will have more experience with these matters.

From my experience, most advisors' reactions fall into one of two extreme categories: 1) angry and refusing to pay anything; or 2) remorseful and wanting to pay any sum to just get the matter settled and over with, regardless of fault. Both of these reactions create problems.

As for the first reaction, anger and refusal to pay, these advisors react aggressively when they first receive the client's or their lawyer's demand letter seeking payment for losses and other damages. They assert that they have no intention of paying any sum to the complainant to resolve the matter, and aggressively state that they didn't do anything wrong.

Then there's the advisor who is too anxious and wants to write a check before the evidence has been collected and reviewed. This is an equally dangerous approach for two reasons. First, if the advisor has errors and omissions insurance, they are not permitted to simply admit culpability and promise payment before the insurance company or insurance broker has had an opportunity to analyze the case and make a determination if payment is appropriate. Second, payment to a client doesn't necessarily mean the matter will be over. The regulator may want to investigate. That could take many months, or sometimes years. The regulator may be pleased on the one hand that the client was reimbursed, but there might be an assumption that you did something wrong if the client receives payment. If you didn't do anything wrong but you conclude with the dealer that a small payment can resolve the complaint, be sure the letter responding to the client complaint a) explores why the allegations are meritless; b) makes clear that the offer of reimbursement, or partial reimbursement, was simply to resolve the matter; and c) encloses a release[5] to be signed by the client before any payment is made. The signed release, particularly one that includes a confidentiality clause, ensures that the client cannot take the money, publicize the settlement, and then begin legal proceedings against you and the dealer.

B. Notify your errors and omissions insurer

The dealer and advisor, if they have insurance, need to put the insurance broker on notice immediately. You should know before you are subject to a complaint whether you have insurance and what it covers.[6] Further, it would be wise to have a dialogue with your broker, in advance of receiving

---

5   Note that the release cannot release the advisor or dealer from any regulatory complaint, as this is also a regulatory infraction. So steer away from including that in the release.

6   I am not an insurance coverage lawyer so you need to contact your insurance broker to find out if you have coverage for the particular complaint. If you are told that you do not have coverage and you want to dispute it, you will have to retain a lawyer with that specialization. Further, many advisors and dealers 'self-insure' (which means no outside insurance policy) and therefore they do not have insurance coverage. You should know before a dispute arises whether you have errors and omissions insurance and what it covers and excludes. Further, your errors and omissions insurer will have an approved list of lawyers they will recommend to you; however, if you want to work with a specific lawyer who has experience in this area you can ask for that person, and if the lawyer is not on the pre-approved list, there may be exceptions made to permit you to use that lawyer.

any complaints, about what would happen if you received a complaint, what triggers coverage, and what you would be expected to communicate to the broker. You will want to know whether you have coverage for legal representation in respect of regulatory matters[7] or whether the coverage applies only for defending against complaining clients. You need to find out whether the coverage extends to legal advice through a regulatory investigation stage or only if you receive a letter asserting allegations. Your insurance broker should help you gain an understanding of your coverage when you sign up, so that you can ensure that you have the right insurance, not just the least expensive one.

If the advisor and dealer have different ideas of how the complaint should proceed or have different interests, there may be a conflict and each may need their own lawyer. This needs to be discussed with your insurance broker at the time the conflict arises to ensure both interests are covered.

Summary

If communication between advisor and client is not both clear and properly documented, the result can be a client complaint, a regulatory probe, or even litigation. Be prepared to avoid mistakes that only make matters worse. In the event of a complaint, maintain emotional composure and report up the ranks to resolve the complaint.

---

7   I have not seen a policy that covers any regulatory penalties imposed by a regulator but some policies cover the legal fees to defend you in regulatory proceedings.

Advisors Take Action

✓ Know whether you have insurance and what it covers in advance of any complaints. If you are insured, discuss with your broker what would happen if you received a complaint, what triggers coverage, and what you would be expected to communicate to the broker.

✓ If a client complains by telephone, ask the client to put their complaint in writing. Say very little, take notes, and keep your emotions in check during the call. Report the call immediately to your branch manager and compliance team.

✓ Do not call or correspond with a client who has sent a complaint letter. Allow your dealer and its compliance team to determine the response. If you are insured, put your broker on notice.

11

The Investigation

THIS CHAPTER WILL equip you with what you need to know—and how and what to communicate—if you get the slightest hint that you might be investigated by the dealer or regulator. You will learn who you need to contact and how to communicate when responding to investigatory requests for documentation and information, whether the request is from your dealer, the regulator, or the OBSI.[1]

I. The Stress Begins

I won't lie, this is going to be an anxious time. But knowing what the process is and what you need to do can help make the stress more manageable.

---

[1]   OBSI is the Ombudsman for Banking Services and Investments; see OBSI.ca for more information.

A. Notifying the SRO/regulator

After a complaint is received, the dealer is obliged to register the complaint with their SRO or the securities regulator.[2] Then the dealer must investigate the matter to prepare its response to the complainant, as well as prepare an investigation report. The regulator either waits for the dealer's report or conducts its own investigation simultaneously.

B. Retaining a lawyer

Advisors can struggle with whether they should get their own lawyer at this stage—or at any stage. They might worry that they need a lawyer to protect their rights because the compliance department or the dealer's in-house lawyers will be looking out for the interests of the dealer rather than protecting advisors.

On the other hand, advisors may also believe that retaining their own lawyer will lead their dealer and/or regulator to think they have something to worry about. Guess what? Advisors do have something to worry about if there is a client complaint, an investigation, and a threat of regulatory sanctions and litigation.

The dealer will decide before, during, or after the investigation whether to penalize the advisor with close or strict supervision, a financial penalty, or, in more serious cases, suspended or terminated registration (or, in the case of insurance agents, terminated employment/agency agreement).

Therefore, an advisor might also worry about the security of their job. If the dealer decides to terminate the advisor's registration, which can be done under most of the agreements at the dealer's whim with just a few weeks' or months' notice,

---

2   See IIROC Rule 3100 and MFDA Policy 6.

the advisor needs to worry about whether their registration will be delayed if they try to transfer to a new dealer. I have seen many advisors stuck in limbo for several months because the regulator wants the investigation of the complaint to be completed before it will register the advisor with a new dealer. Meanwhile, the advisor risks losing their book of business as the clients need to be serviced, usually by someone at the dealer from which the advisor is departing.

Is all of this scary? You bet! Should you retain your own counsel? If you want to push the regulator to move more quickly, a lawyer can assist. If you are going to be interviewed by the regulator to determine whether you should be registered, you need to retain a lawyer to prepare you for the interview and attend with you because there is a lot at stake. Don't worry that the regulator will think you are guilty of something just because you have a lawyer with you. The regulator often prefers that advisors have lawyers in the interview to ensure there is the perception of "fairness," given that there is usually a lawyer in the room representing the regulator. Further, the interview will likely proceed more efficiently if the advisor is represented and prepared in advance to answer questions directly.

On most occasions in which a regulator is investigating an advisor for an infraction or for a transfer of license, there is an exchange of letters between the regulator and the advisor.[3] The letters from the regulator mostly include a series of questions, which the advisor must respond to in writing. The advisor may need to retain a lawyer to assist with the preparation of the response.

---

3   Letters from the regulator may be addressed to the dealer and then the dealer collects answers from the advisor. In that case, all answers are provided by the advisor and given to the dealer, and then passed by the dealer to the regulator.

If you do decide to retain a lawyer, you need to know the following:

1. Do you have errors and omissions insurance? If the advisor does have coverage, depending on the policy, legal fees may be paid for by the insurance. Note that an investigation can be triggered by other things, such as an audit that reveals a regulatory infraction, for which the advisor might also need a lawyer. You need to inquire whether your errors and omissions insurance covers circumstances in which there isn't a client complaint and the matter has not been referred to the enforcement department of the regulator.[4]

2. Your relationship with your own lawyer is confidential.[5] You don't have an obligation to inform your dealer that you retained your own lawyer, although many dealers suggest that the advisor retain a separate lawyer. Anything you tell your lawyer, and all materials that pass between you and your lawyer, are completely confidential, unless you direct your lawyer to share such information with the dealer, regulator, client, or someone else.

3. Lawyers are expensive! You know this one already. If there is no insurance coverage, legal advice is expensive. If the advisor retains their own lawyer, they will have to pay

---

4   While I am retained by errors and omissions insurers regularly, I am not a lawyer with expertise on the issue of insurance coverage, so this book does not go into a detailed review of what is covered or not; for that you need an insurance coverage legal expert and usually your insurance broker can explain this very well to you. So hopefully you don't need a lawyer for that.

5   The legal term is 'privileged'; there are books written on this subject that are beyond the content of this book.

for that lawyer. If the dealer retains a lawyer who is supposed to represent both dealer and advisor, the terms of the advisor's contract with the dealer will dictate who pays. Therefore, if the advisor retains an outside lawyer separately from the dealer, the advisor risks being stuck with the legal fees for both his own lawyer and the dealer's lawyer.[6] However, if there is errors and ommissions insurance and a conflict of interest exists or arises, contact your insurance broker to determine whether it is possible that the policy will cover both lawyers' fees.

II. The Investigation: What to Expect

First, the advisor needs to know that the dealer's and regulator's investigations can be conducted simultaneously. All information and tone reflected in emails will potentially impact both the dealer's and the regulator's investigations. All the more reason to get this right. Here are some of the dos and don'ts.

A. Co-operation: delivering the documents

You can ask compliance or legal what they need from you to assist with the response to the complaint. Do this in a calm and collected manner. The strength and weaknesses of the response are almost always dependent on one thing: the strength of the advisor's paper trail. In the simple example of

---

6   While employment law is not the focus of this book and will not be explored, it is important to review the offer letter carefully before signing as these provisions are set out therein and are often overlooked by the advisor. I represent advisors and dealers in employment/agency litigation so I have reviewed employment/agency agreements/letters with advisors both before and after they have been signed, and they are often surprised at the fact that they may be responsible for the dealer's legal fees.

Mrs. Koo, the contemporaneous[7] notes taken by the advisor to prove the client's risk profile at the time the investments were made will be absolutely and fundamentally key. Letters, notes of telephone calls, and emails are all crucial.[8]

The advisor needs to co-operate with the dealer to assist with the collection of the documents and the preparation of the response. No lawyer is needed for this step, as the paper trail prepared throughout the relationship is what it is. It all gets shared with the dealer and the regulator.

B. Answering questions in writing

After documents are received by the dealer and sent to the regulator, the advisor may receive written questions to answer in writing. But before you prepare your answers for the investigation, you first need to appreciate the source of the questions and where the answers are likely to go.

The investigation is sometimes conducted by the dealer and regulator simultaneously. That means that while the dealer's head-office staff might be asking questions, the regulator might be asking questions as well. Simultaneously, the regulator might be writing to the dealer's head office asking questions. While the regulator could ask questions of the advisor directly through an email or letter, as mentioned, frequently the regulator writes to the dealer with questions to be directed to the advisor.

The initial source of the questions is immaterial because,

---

7   Contemporaneous notes are prepared at the same time as the events occurred, not after the complaint was made, based on advisor's best recollection. See also *Advisor at Risk*, page 97.

8   For more on note-taking, see *Advisor at Risk*, which explores this in depth.

ultimately, the dealer shares its investigation report with the regulator, likely including the supporting documents and information collected from you. Regardless of whether the dealer or the regulator is asking the questions, all answers provided by the advisor should be prepared with utmost care, assuming these will be provided, for better or worse, to the regulator.

This is more difficult than the collection of documents. While the paper trail is whatever it is and cannot be altered, the answers are prepared and subject to judgment. The answers you provide need to be thought through carefully, as each question and answer can come back to haunt you if it isn't:

- 100% truthful;
- 100% accurate; and
- 100% consistent with the paper trail.

What does that mean?

1. No guessing!
2. No rambling on into areas not being asked about. Stick with the answer to the question asked.

In sum, it means directly, truthfully, and accurately answering the questions.

Advisors have trouble with this step because they tend to ramble into areas unrelated to the questions asked by the regulator. When someone is nervous, they may not do a good job of preparing answers that might have significant and potentially detrimental consequences to themselves and their livelihood. If I had to write something that I knew was for the regulator who was judging whether I could continue to practice law, and this could potentially impact my reputation, you can be sure that I would not send it to the regulator without getting legal advice, regardless of the cost. Lawyers have a saying: "A man who is his own lawyer has a fool for a client."[9] This also applies to advisors and dealers who prepare written answers for their regulator without getting legal advice.[10] If the in-house compliance officers or lawyers are keen to assist the advisor, that can be helpful as long as they are aligned and not in any conflict. Even so, advisors can quietly retain their own lawyer as a second set of eyes to ensure their interests are being protected.

It's also prudent to expect that any written answers provided to the compliance or legal department are likely going to be shared with the regulator. If the questions are directed by the regulator to the dealer to ask the advisor, the dealer may leave the advisor to their own devices to prepare the answers, with no support or assistance. These are the very answers that are almost always shared with the regulator. This is a huge problem because the advisor doesn't appreciate how important it is for these answers to be accurate. Advisors tend to either a) take the matter too lightly, not thinking their answers through the way an experienced lawyer would, or b) get tangled up in the answer and ramble on too much. The result is usually bad for the advisor, who may be later challenged about

---

9   While this proverb first began appearing in print in the early 19th century, its precise origin is unknown. See www.phrases.org.uk.

10   In-house lawyers and experienced compliance officers usually have this expertise and are usually well equipped to prepare these answers on behalf of their dealers, but even these qualified professionals should pass the draft to outside litigation lawyers for a quick look before sending it to a regulator, as an ounce of prevention—a step that is inexpensive and worthwhile.

the accuracy of the response, or even accused of being dishonest or evasive. In fairness, advisors don't have the training necessary.

I see these questions and answers when I am (finally) retained, either if there is a regulatory examination (improperly called an "interview") or if there is litigation. These answers are almost always very (and I really mean VERY) damaging to the advisor. Many times the advisor believes they are answering the question truthfully, but the answers turn out to be incorrect, opening up several other cans of worms.

Here is a simple example of a question that might be asked:

REGULATOR: It appears that the complainant, Mrs. Koo, signed her KYC form before you inserted the information. Have you done this with other clients? If so, please identify them by name.

ADVISOR, WITHOUT LEGAL ADVICE: No, I have never done this, other than for Mrs. Koo.

First, has the advisor done a review of Mrs. Koo's file to see if indeed she signed the KYC before the form was entirely completed? A careful review could potentially show that this didn't happen and that Mrs. Koo is lying. Or there is a reason why she believes this to be the case but she is wrong.

Second, has the advisor done a full audit of their files to determine whether there are any other blank signed forms, or emails, faxes, or letters in any client file that indicate such a process was indeed followed on other occasions?

If there is a tight deadline to respond, I would suggest the following answer:

I would like the opportunity to review Mrs. Koo's file as I do not recall sending her a blank signed form. That was not my practice. I will need a few days to review carefully.

Further, as for any other client KYC forms, I would like to carefully review the other files, as I do not recall following this practice. I want to be certain before I answer "no" that indeed there are no others. I will need a week to respond. Certainly, if you have evidence of any other documents of concern, please direct me to those documents and I will review those files first.

If it was the advisor's practice to get clients to sign blank forms, we would have to dig down to find out why the advisor proceeded in this fashion, and attempt to provide an explanation. While it is a problem to follow this process, it exacerbates the problem to lie about it. Lying may end in termination and additional regulatory penalties.

C. Oral examination by the dealer or regulator

While the dealer's examination is commonly referred to as a 'meeting' and the regulator's examination is called an 'interview', you need to be prepared to be cross-examined. All of your answers can be used against you. The dealer may fire you and the regulator may penalize you, or suspend or revoke your license permanently. While you need to co-operate and answer all questions, the consequences may be dire. Don't be naive. I am telling it to you straight.

I am not going to go into detail to describe the preparation required for such a 'meeting' or 'interview'. But not preparing is akin to attending an oral final exam in which your university degree hinges on you passing without studying.

Some of the regulators believe that an element of surprise is going to evoke the most honest answers. I couldn't disagree more! Being asked questions in a vacuum without the opportunity to review files and documents is completely unacceptable and unfair. All that to say, any advisor, compliance officer, branch manager, president, Ultimate Designated Person (UDP), or anyone else who doesn't seek legal advice to prepare them for a regulatory interview—or even a discussion with the regulator—does not value their license or does not appreciate that their license is at risk.

III. Post Investigation

Once the investigation is complete, there are many decisions to make that an advisor will need to consider carefully.

A. Avenues for the client complaint: the OBSI

If a client is complaining about losses of less than the amount mandated by the OBSI and the client finds the dealer's response unsatisfactory, a complaint can be brought to the OBSI.

Clients do not need to hire lawyers for this process. Many investors approach my office for legal advice and we send most of them away. However, advisors interviewed by the OBSI need a lawyer's support to prepare, for the same reasons they need help with their response to written and oral questions in an investigation by a dealer.

Because a claim has been launched, errors and omissions insurance, if you have it, could include coverage of your legal costs to prepare. Regardless, it is important to hire a lawyer with industry experience. In an OBSI matter, in contrast to an investigation by the dealer, there is usually no conflict between advisor and dealer. This is because the advisor appears both on behalf of themselves and on behalf of the dealer at an OBSI interview. While there are exceptions,[11] the dealer and advisor are almost always on the same side in an OBSI investigation.

The OBSI will interview the client and the advisor and review the documentation. The OBSI investigators will formulate an opinion and write to both the advisor's dealer and the client, advising whether the dealer should be responsible to reimburse the client for any portion of the loss.

Many dealers have complained to me that the OBSI's findings are always averse to the dealer. I believe that part of the problem is that no one prepares the advisor for the interview, so the advisor is blindsided by the questions. I have prepared advisors and the results have been more favorable to the dealer because the advisor is better prepared, less stressed, and answers questions more thoroughly, directly, and accurately.

One such advisor wrote: "Having you prepare me for the OBSI interview helped me immensely in my case. You helped me summarize the facts that were pertinent to my case. You sat down with me and ran through what I should expect. So, during the interview, I was able to answer questions in a clearer and more concise way. I found that this assistance was extremely helpful and it was one of the reasons that the OBSI sided with me."

The OBSI told the client he had no case against the dealer and advisor. Was this an expensive exercise? Yes, it is expensive to hire a lawyer, but good value compared to having to pay as much as $350,000[12] to the client. Of course, there are no guarantees that retaining a lawyer will lead the OBSI to

---

11 A conflict most commonly occurs when the advisor is no longer registered with the dealer.

12 At the time of writing, the limit of OBSI's authority is $350,000.

dismiss the case, but even if it is your view that the case has no merit, don't go in cold to the interview.

The OBSI cannot penalize or impose a settlement. The only thing it can do is go public with its finding, naming the dealer and publicizing its investigation findings and conclusions in detail.[13] The threat is to tarnish reputations. If the dealer or advisor want to avoid this "name and shame" tactic, then they can settle with the client for the amount the OBSI is suggesting, or a lesser sum if the client agrees.

Assuming the amount of the claim is higher than the mandate of the OBSI, or the dealer and advisor cannot settle with the client, the client's next step could be litigation.

B. When clients sue

Litigation is a fancy word for suing.[14] Unless there are substantial losses at issue, litigation is not the appropriate choice for a client because the legal bills received from their own lawyer will likely far exceed the sum of their losses.[15]

Regardless of the sum sought by the client, litigation causes tremendous stress for the advisor. That is why the advisor and dealer often opt to pay the client to resolve these matters, even if they think the client is wrong and the advisor is right. The legal costs can mount up very quickly to more than what the client was asking for in the first place. More importantly, one

---

13   Readers: keep a close eye on this; there are proposals underway to give OBSI more power—and even make it completely enforceable.

14   See *Advisor at Risk*, Chapter 11.

15   Some jurisdictions permit lawyers to work on a contingency basis for a suing client, taking a percentage of the payment ultimately made to the client, either through out of court settlement or trial judgment. However, the losses must be significant for a lawyer to take the matter on that basis, as the risk is high that the plaintiff's action could drag on for a long time and that the claim has little or no merit at the end of the trial.

needs to factor in the stress and distraction caused by a lawsuit when determining whether to pay to settle the matter or fight.

C. To pay or not to pay, that is the question

If you have errors and omissions insurance, the decision on whether to resolve matters at an early stage or fight the claim may be mostly out of your hands. If there is no errors and omission insurance, then the dealer may be making the decision. It is likely set out in the employment or agency agreement whether the dealer is permitted to settle most complaints and then collect the settlement paid, along with any legal fees, from the advisor. If it is not in the agreement, then it is ripe for discussion.

However, if it is decided that the complaint has little or no merit or that the sum sought is unreasonable, it is likely that the response to the complaint will be to deny the claim, regardless of who is calling the shots. The letter responding to the complaint may indicate what the investigation revealed about the allegations and why these are in dispute.

According to most regulatory requirements, all complaints must be dealt with effectively, fairly, and expeditiously.[16] Since the regulator ultimately sees the response, it needs to be thorough and include a reasonable assessment of the merits. Otherwise, the dealer could be faced with complaint-handling charges by the regulator.[17]

If the matter is not resolved early on, the complaint will likely continue for some lengthy period of time—months and

---

16 See IIROC Rule 2500B for more details, or MFDA Policy 3 or CSA Notice of Amendments to N.I. 31-103 and Companion Policy 31-103CP.

17 See IIROC Rule 3100 and MFDA Policy 6.

sometimes years. Regardless of whether the complaint is resolved early in the process or continues, the regulator will investigate the matter, and determine whether to close it with a warning or cautionary letter, or to pursue to a hearing and ultimately penalize the advisor, branch manager, and/or dealer.[18]

D. The powers of the regulator

What if the matter goes from the regulator's investigation department to the enforcement department? Quite separate from litigation, when a client issues a complaint to the regulator, and the regulator finds there is evidence of a regulatory infraction, it can escalate the matter to its enforcement department.

The enforcement department can commence proceedings seeking severe penalties, including financial penalties, or suspension or revocation of the advisor's license. While the regulator can seek costs of the investigation against the registrant if it wins, the registrant cannot seek its own costs from the regulator if the regulator is unsuccessful.

While an SRO does not have authority to compel an advisor or dealer to compensate a client, it sometimes uses its powers indirectly. If the regulator concludes that there was no client harm, or that the client was made whole with a payment by the dealer or the advisor, this can be factored into the penalty.

However, until recently, IIROC and the MFDA were not permitted to enforce in court the penalties ordered by the MFDA or IIROC tribunals. Certain provinces have granted them authority to directly register and enforce disciplinary

---

18   For more details on the steps in litigation and regulatory proceedings, see *Advisor at Risk*, Chapters 11 and 12.

decisions with the court so that these penalties can be collected from advisors and dealers who have left the industry.[19]

E. Reputational damage

No one likes to have their name in the paper or precedents of their case referred to for decades after a trial or regulatory hearing. Very few cases go to trial; this is usually because one or both parties loses steam or runs out of money. But the most significant impetus to settlement is embarrassment or the potential for reputational damage. There are judgments in which the judge specifically indicates that an advisor or client was not believable or was lying. No one likes to be judged in that manner. Putting yourself out there, taking the witness stand, leaves both client and advisor/dealer vulnerable to a conclusion that will be public information forever. Advisors and dealers are very concerned, to say the least, about reputational damage associated with a public trial or hearing. This is enough of an impetus to settle the case before trial.

While a settlement out of court can be kept private, a regulatory settlement is public, so the matter remains on the internet for years. Therefore, if most client complaints are as a result of a breakdown in communication, the threat of reputational damage alone should be sufficient incentive to improve this aspect of your relationship with clients. That has been the purpose of this book: to show you that much danger lies in the communication gap, to help you close that gap, and to avoid the stress and reputational damage that inevitably results from a client complaint.

---

19   At the time of writing, this power has been granted to several of the provinces. For more information, see the Babin Bessner Spry LLP blog at www.babinbessnerspry .com/blog/more-legal-authority-to-industry-regulators.html.

Summary

An advisor under investigation by a dealer, regulator, or the OBSI has a lot at stake, risking dealer penalties, loss of job security, regulatory sanctions, and reputational damage. It is crucial that advisors seek appropriate legal assistance and representation in the event of an investigation.

Advisors Take Action

✓ Co-operate with your dealer to assist with the collection of documents and the preparation of your response to the complaint. Remember, the strength of your paper trail determines the strength of your response.

✓ Answer all written questions directly, truthfully, and accurately. Don't ramble. Have a lawyer review your answers to ensure your interests are being protected.

✓ Obtain legal advice to prepare for any oral examination by your dealer, the regulator, or the OBSI.

Conclusion

IT STRUCK ME after writing my first book, *Advisor at Risk*, that I had another important message for advisors to help them protect themselves and the valued book of business that they have worked so hard to grow. That message is that advisors need to take the time to work through any and all communication gaps with clients to build a healthier and more remunerative business. Writing this book has been a labor of love, one that has taken over my weekends and holidays for more than three years. I hope that my message has come through, and that the information and advice in this book will prove valuable and rewarding for you and your client relationships.

The guide for clients, which accompanies this book (see page 246) is available for download online. The client guide is designed for your clients, to help them understand and fulfill their own role in bridging the gap and ensuring a rewarding relationship. After all, if the client is satisfied with the relationship, you will have a healthier book of business that will surely grow through referrals.

Many advisors are fearful of reading my books and attending my seminars. But judging from the numbers of those who do attend and who have purchased my first book, the courageous are clearly a large group. If you have come this far in reading this book, you are certainly among them. I urge you to continue to tap into this courage, and to refer back to this book as often as needed to enact and maintain my suggestions with a renewed energy. The case studies and examples I have laid out, as well as the headings and checklists within each chapter, were designed to make the book easy to navigate and easy to come back to as a future reference. However, to condense my central messages into one simple and brief list, let me conclude with this. You can bridge the communication gap by:

1. Understanding how communication gaps occur and closing these gaps to reduce your risk.

2. Understanding yourself, what your own gaps are, and whether you can close them by either developing your communication skills or surrounding yourself with a team that complements your strengths and fills in the gaps of your weaknesses.

3. Valuing and working hard to earn your clients' trust, allowing them to be transparent with you so that you can ensure the product choices are suitable.

4. Appreciating your Know Your Product obligations and explaining complexities to clients, whether those clients are sophisticated or not.

5. Planning for clients in a manner that reflects your obligations.

6. Approaching women and senior clients with an appreciation of the risks of getting it wrong.

If you want to delve more into this and related subjects, please subscribe to my regular articles. You can do so by emailing me at ebessner@babinbessnerspry.com.

Again, in a world where building a business is hard, and keeping a business is harder, I sincerely hope that you find this book helpful—along with *Advisor at Risk*. The instructions both books offer have been designed to help you build a fruitful career and an improved relationship with your clients.

GOOD LUCK, AND all the best to you.

—ELLEN

How to get copies of *Investor's Guide*

I wrote the following companion guide to help your clients understand how to communicate better with you. After all, it takes two to build an effective working relationship. With the purchase of *Communication Risk,* you are entitled to download free printable copies at BabinBessnerSpry.com using the code **bessnerdn.** Feel free to share this resource with all your clients!

COMMUNICATION RISK

INVESTOR'S GUIDE

How to Get the Most from Your Registered Advisor

ELLEN BESSNER

BABIN BESSNER SPRY LLP

A Guide for Investors to Bridge the Client-Advisor Communication Gap

A QUALIFIED ADVISOR IS there for an investor like you: someone who wants to be set up for financial success but needs professional advice to get there. How can you make sure you are getting the most from your relationship with your advisor? The answer is in one word: **Communication**.

Even the best advisors cannot predict what financial markets will do. But what they can do is help you set reasonable goals based on history—yours and the market's. A registered advisor can help you articulate what you want to achieve, draw up a plan to get there, and then—this is key—steer you through market shifts, helping you stick to your plan in good times and bad. If you don't have clear goals and a clear investment plan, you run the risk of being overcome by fear and selling when markets fall.

The more well suited your plan is to your needs, and the better your advisor understands your risk profile and ability to ride out market spikes and dips, the more likely you are to achieve your objectives. This is where communication comes in. Your advisor must help you see what's possible (and what isn't), work with you to set reasonable goals, get to know what level of risk you are able to live with, and make sure you understand your plan and investments. The key to getting the most from your advisor is clear, open communication from the outset about who you are, how you live, and what you want. Between the two of you, you can close the communication gap.

In my role as a lawyer, I have seen the results of relationships gone bad, mostly due to investors being disappointed about not having met their expectations and blaming their advisors. This often leads to complaints (to the investment firm and even to regulators), stress, and significant costs. I wrote this booklet to help you avoid this situation by revealing the importance of frank two-way communication between you and your advisor. The more open you are about your spending habits, finances, career, and personal life, the better your advisor can help you achieve your financial goals, and the more likely you are to achieve success.

I'm going to show you how you can foster this openness, what you should expect from your advisor, and how to work with your advisor to ensure that they hold up their end in the relationship.

The Benefits of Working with an Advisor

At some point, many people would benefit from professional help with their money, whether it is to set priorities during high-earning and high-cost years or to prepare for retirement. A registered advisor can:

- keep you on track when financial markets are volatile,
- temper your enthusiasm to buy when markets are rising, and
- calm your nerves when markets inevitably fall and remind you to stay the course.

Studies have shown that people who get professional investment advice achieve greater net worth because they avoid common behavioral investment errors. Why? Because their advisor helps them stick to their investment program, and sticking to your plan is an important factor for financial success.[1]

---

1   http://www.ific.ca/wp-content/uploads/2013/09/IFIC-Value-of-Advice-Report-2011-November-2011 .pdf/4000/ at pages 1, 5, and 9.

Why "Registered"?

I want to emphasize the word registered. Many of the problems that arise between investors and some so-called "advisors" involve those who allege to be experts in the financial services industry but are not registered, and they are not licensed to sell the products they are selling.

Registered advisors answer to government bodies that have the job of watching them and making sure they have the necessary proficiencies and are acting within the rules and in your interests. If they don't, they can be penalized publicly. It is important to verify that your advisor is actually registered with a provincial securities commission, the Mutual Fund Dealers Association of Canada (MFDA), or the Investment Industry Regulatory Organization of Canada (IIROC). If your advisor sells you insurance, they must be registered with the licensing organization in your province.

A Professional Partnership

Registered advisors are professionals, like lawyers, doctors, dentists, or accountants. In the same way you might seek out a doctor with whom you feel comfortable and can trust, you should also seek out a suitable advisor who will take the time to understand your needs and goals. You and your advisor should sit on the same side of the table, working together as partners to achieve your financial goals.

What You Bring to the Table

A good advisor will bring a solid understanding of investment markets and products and a genuine desire to help you achieve your goals. But what do you, the client, bring?

If you want the relationship to result in success, you must deliver three critical things:

1. **Honesty and transparency:** Sometimes investors are reluctant to tell their advisors about their income, their assets, or their financial obligations. Other times, investors claim to be more comfortable with market dips than they really are. To enter into a partnership, you must be willing to give your advisor all the information they need—and they do need it—to fully understand your goals, risk profile, and what investments will be most suitable for you at different points in time. These things will change with your circumstances, so you must keep your advisor updated throughout the relationship. Without this information, your advisor will not be able to do the best job for you. Being open and honest, both with your advisor and with yourself, lays the foundation of trust that is so essential to a successful partnership.

2. **Openness:** Express yourself: your hopes and fears, your dreams and aspirations, how you feel about money, and your views about investing. Were you in the stock market during the last big meltdown? If so, how did it feel? Did you sell or hang on? Helping your advisor understand how you see things will let them pick investments more suitably aligned with your risk profile.

3. **Regular contact:** Keep your advisor informed about every change that comes your way—for better or worse—that might impact your financial situation. As an investor, sometimes it can be easy to forget to call, or sometimes you may feel embarrassed about life events that could affect your financial plans: a lost job, a sudden debt, even a divorce. These are important events to share with your advisor. Your advisor is your partner and can help you adjust your investments to meet unexpected short-term needs, and then help you get back on track for the future. If you do not tell your advisor about your changed financial circumstances, you are not going to get the help and support that you need during difficult times. On the other side of the coin, maybe you will receive a bonus, promotion, new job, or an inheritance. Some investors keep this to themselves, for fear of being pressured to "hand it all over." But if your advisor doesn't know about it, they can't help you use it to meet your goals. Don't want to hand it all over? Just

tell them you want to keep a chunk of it. You deserve it! Your advisor is not there to grab your money or make you feel ashamed or embarrassed. Your advisor is there to serve you. But they cannot serve you properly if you are not transparent.

Keep in mind that it is your advisor's duty to find out about your financial circumstances—there are even regulations specifically about this area, called the Know Your Client rule. So if your advisor seems to be pressing you for information, don't consider this invasive. Instead, know that they are looking out for your interests and meeting regulatory obligations. If you aren't providing information, and your advisor is not trying to dig deeper, that is when you should start to wonder.

How to Have an Advisor as a Partner

Creating a partnership with your advisor starts with setting the right foundation for the relationship. Follow these three steps to make sure that your foundation is solid.

Step I: Dos and Don'ts

If you are just looking to buy the latest hot stock, you may be better off using an online or discount broker. But, increasingly, investors are seeking help with financial planning, which might include investment, tax, retirement, and estate planning. If this is you, take your time, reflect on what you want out of the relationship, and choose carefully. I have explained why you need to be open and transparent with your advisor, but that relationship is a two-way street. Here are some Dos and Don'ts to ensure your advisor is going to be a true partner for you in meeting your financial goals.

DO	DON'T
✔ Choose an advisor with whom you feel comfortable and who you feel has the competencies and services you need.	✘ Don't choose your advisor on personality alone. As with any professional—a doctor, for example—your advisor must be competent, not just a pleasant person.
✔ Consider in advance what you want, and do not want, from an advisor. Do you want a financial plan, annual or semi-annual meetings, a diversified portfolio, or certain types of investments?	✘ Don't change advisors before you: a) explain why you are dissatisfied, b) give them a chance to tell you why you have not met your goals, and c) consider the cost of moving to a different advisor.
✔ Choose an advisor with whom you feel you can share your personal information, history, and concerns.	✘ Don't be passive or silent, or accept an advisor who talks too much and doesn't listen or probe into what you are saying and what you mean.
✔ Express your expectations. Be transparent about whether you know what your needs and wants are. Be flexible, and open to suggestions, as a good advisor might hit the nail on the head in a way you never considered but that makes sense to you.	✘ Don't be embarrassed to ask questions.
✔ Consider whether your expectations are different from your life partner's/spouse's, and ensure the advisor can accommodate any differing expectations. Consider whether a joint investment account with your partner/spouse is appropriate if you have completely different risk profiles.	✘ Don't be afraid to tell your advisor that you are leaving because they don't treat you as an individual if they only speak to your spouse/partner.
✔ Choose an advisor with whom you feel comfortable asking questions and who answers your questions clearly and directly. Tell your advisor what you know and don't know so that they can explain things appropriately.	✘ Don't accept answers that you do not understand, including acronyms or industry terms. An advisor should never make you feel stupid about any questions you ask.

✔ Learn to read your statements so that you can understand what you are investing in and how your investments are performing. Open and review all mail you receive, and get your advisor to teach you what is more and less important.	✘ Don't pick an advisor who tells you not to bother reading anything.
✔ Develop criteria to judge your advisor, such as whether milestones are set and whether you achieve them.	✘ Don't prejudge your advisor based solely on the returns of your investments. It is also important to consider the goals you set.
✔ Always ask your advisor what level of service you can expect with a portfolio like yours, and whether your portfolio is too small to get proper service.[2] It might be better to open a discount or robo account until you have saved a certain sum. You can also explain to your advisor your plan to reach their minimum balance.[3]	✘ Don't assume that every advisor will service small accounts.
✔ Consider value, and whether you believe the advisor can help you formulate a plan to meet your financial goals.	✘ Don't just go for the advisor with the least expensive fee or commission structure.
✔ Ask how the communication and coordination with other professionals (e.g., lawyers, accountants, insurance agents, or portfolio managers and planners) will be carried out, depending on your advisor's certifications for the services provided.	✘ Don't believe anyone who says they can time or predict the market. No one in this industry has a crystal ball.
✔ Develop milestones for one, three, five years or more, and assess regularly whether these are being achieved.	✘ Don't be too rigid about short-term returns. Remember, a market cycle can be three to five years long and it wouldn't be fair to judge your advisor until at least one cycle has passed.

2 "The financial advice industry's bad client problem," by Rob Carrick, *Globe and Mail,* January 30, 2017.
3 *Ibid.*

Step II: Discussion Points for Success

Now that you understand the Dos and Don'ts, allow me to suggest the following considerations to discuss with your advisor to set up the relationship for success.[4]

1. **What is your advisor licensed to sell?** Find out what products the advisor is licensed to sell and what they are not permitted to sell.

2. **Do they have additional certifications?** Do they have additional qualifications, like financial or tax planning certification, or are they also a certified accountant?

3. **Are they experienced?** Have they worked with people like you before, in terms of age, assets, or any particular requirements? Do they have the necessary experience to address your particular issues and goals?

4. **How are they compensated?** Ask how they get paid and how it is calculated. If you feel uncomfortable bringing it up, bring this guide and use it to break the ice. Remember that the least expensive option is not necessarily the best value. Consider what they are bringing to the table.

5. **What are their resources?** Ask the advisor which dealer or company they are affiliated with or licensed through. You will want to know their resources, who else is on the team, what role they play, how much access you will have to the advisor, how often they will meet with you, and for what purpose.

6. **What are the logistics associated with meetings?** If your advisor is far from you, consider how you will be able to arrange meetings, and factor that into your decision.

---

4   These points have been adapted from "Seven criteria for finding the right advisor," by Brenda Bouw, *Globe and Mail*, February 10, 2017.

7. **What is their process?** Ask what process they will follow to develop and meet your goals. If this is an existing relationship and your advisor has not yet made this clear, ask them to make it clear now.

Step III: Maintaining the Relationship

Now that you have established a solid foundation on which to build your client-advisor relationship, the final step is to develop and maintain good communication practices. This involves a little bit of effort and presence of mind, but it is critical to the long-term success of the partnership.

Setting Reasonable, Measurable Goals

If you are transparent, and your advisor is transparent with you, the two of you (often together with a planner, accountant, and potentially other advisors) will establish goals, along with a roadmap for meeting them. It is both of your jobs to make sure the goals are reasonable and measurable.

Let's say you and your advisor set a measurable goal to save and invest a specified sum each month, with a forecasted average return per year over five years. The important thing is not how your investments are doing right now, or a week after you make the investment, but instead whether you are on track to meet those longer term goals.[5] You can assess progress periodically to determine if both you and your advisor are working in tandem to meet your objectives. If not, you might have to make some adjustments which should be discussed with your advisor.

Be Committed to Your Plan

Once you have a financial plan, don't throw it in a drawer to collect dust. Your advisor should not do this, either. Keep yourself in line by managing your savings, spending, and debt according to what you set out in your plan. Meet with your advisor at least once a year to review the plan and the underlying assumptions to ensure you are still on track.

---

5   "The financial advice industry's bad client problem," by Rob Carrick, *Globe and Mail,* Jan. 30, 2017.

Don't Rush, or Be Rushed

Your advisor is responsible for understanding you and for making a plan that is suitable to you and your needs and goals. You are responsible for investing the time it takes to make sure your advisor can be effective. You both need to allow time for:

- letting your advisor get to know your values and financial situation so they can determine your risk profile and objectives,

- thinking through and determining what questions you need to ask,

- allowing your advisor the opportunity to explain product features and costs, and how certain products will contribute to meeting your goals; if you don't understand your investments, you cannot judge whether they are the right fit for you, and

- reading and understanding any material your advisor gives you. Sometimes these can be confusing, so keep asking questions.

Remember, you must take as much time as you need to understand what your advisor is telling you and showing you—and, in turn, your advisor needs to give you that time and make sure you are communicating together effectively.

A Last Word on Transparency in Communication

I've mentioned transparency several times, and I'll mention it here once more. Why? Because it is critical for a successful client-advisor relationship, and transparency goes both ways.

Meeting your goals, through a financial plan or otherwise, can only be achieved with effective communication between you and your advisor. If you hold back information, including private and personal details, your advisor cannot properly assess your goals or help you plan for a successful future.

Let's say you don't want to share information about your income and spending habits. Your advisor will not be able to accurately determine how much you can afford to save, how much money you need to cover costs in the short or long term, and how much you need to meet larger goals, such as saving to buy a house, for retirement, or for any succession plan associated with what you would like to leave your beneficiaries after your passing.

Remember, you are paying for your advisor's service, and they can't provide that service if they don't have the facts. Whatever your spending obligations or habits, admit it. If you are afraid to divulge your income because you don't want to be pressured to save more, then say so. Your advisor can only build a meaningful plan if they understand your limitations. A plan built on untruths will be useless to you, or worse.

If you don't want to share information with your advisor for the simple reason that it is personal, tell them this, up front, rather than being evasive or misleading. But don't be surprised if they try to persuade you to change your mind. Their job is to know these details so they can help you meet your goals.

What's Next?

Do you have concerns about your advisor? If so, call them and ask to discuss the points raised in this booklet. By opening up the lines of communication, you may be able to reframe your relationship and move forward more successfully.

Remember, switching advisors costs money. If you find yourself jumping from one advisor to another, consider your side of the relationship. Are you contributing to the failure of the relationship without realizing it? Assess the advice in this booklet and consider whether you might be undermining your chances for financial success by not being transparent about your situation, your needs, your habits, and your goals.

Investors Take Action

How does this all sum up? Whether you are working with someone new or rebuilding an existing relationship, here's what you need to do to fulfill your end in developing a successful client-advisor partnership:

✓ Get involved, participate, and meet your advisor halfway.

✓ Examine your relationship with money, and be transparent about it with yourself and your advisor, so together you can shape a plan to meet your goals.

✓ Work with your advisor to bridge the communication gap—both ways!—so that you can reach your own financial success.

Index

A

Advisor at Risk (Bessner), 1

advisors: author's experience with, 72-75; common defenses by, 19-25; gender imbalance, 164-65; nature of professional relationship with, 10-12, 21-22; references, 35-36; responsibility to understand client, 20-21, 24, 41, 76-77. *See also* clients; communication gap; complaints; investigations

advisors, knowing self: introduction and summary, 45, 65; action steps, 66; benefits from, 47; brand messaging, 64-65; business awareness and changes, 57, 64; case study (Smee), 45-46, 50-51, 54; client turnover, 58-59; lack of awareness about risks, 53-56; licenses and certifications, 57-58; payment models, 62-63; risk profile (risk tolerance), 52-53, 56; services rendered, 61-62; strengths, weaknesses, likes, and dislikes exercise, 47-52; target market, 58-59; teams, 63-64; travel and location, 60-61

age, client, 119-20

agenda, 107-8

apologies, 214-15

asset concerns, 38

B

background, client, 117-18

best interest: power of attorney and, 195-96; use of term, 65n13

Boston Consulting Group, 165, 170, 171, 172, 173, 175

boundaries, 60n10

brand messaging, 64-65

Bunny, Mr. and Mrs. (women clients case study), 162-63, 167, 168-69, 180

business, *see* advisors, knowing self

C

capacity/incapacity, 189-92

capital preservation, 198

cash, 100-101

certifications and licenses, 57-58

change: in advisor's business, 52n2, 57, 64; client capacity/incapacity, 189-92; in client's life, 71, 75, 133; financial planning and, 146-47, 158-59; KYC form updates, 86-90, 133n9

Client Relationship Model (CRM), 11n4, 62n12

clients: introduction and summary, 67, 90; action steps, 90-91; assessment of, 34-35; asset concerns, 38; changes in lives of, 71, 75, 133, 146-47; deception by, 85; engagement by, 32–33, 80–83, 107, 158; explaining investment products to, 103–4, 107–11; face value issues, 13–15; KYC form updates, 86–90, 133n9; lack of understanding and responsibility for investments, 40–41, 80, 83–84; listening to, 70, 73–74, 77–80, 117, 170; mistrust of advisors, 39; privacy issues, 38, 153, 188–89; probing for information, 36–38; problem solving for, 71; referrals from, 68, 75, 166–67; revolving door with, 68; secrecy and misrepresentation, 15–16, 29, 39; servicing practices, 69–71; strong foundations with, 68–69; transparency from, 84; trial period with, 35; turning away or letting go, 56, 71, 86; turnover, 58–59; understanding the client, 20–21, 24, 41, 76–77. *See also* complaints; Know Your Client (KYC) form; risk profile, clients

communication gap: introduction and summary, 1–2, 2–3, 5, 25, 244–45; accepting clients at face value, 13–15; action steps, 26; case studies, 5–10; secrecy and lack of trust, 15–16; unreasonable expectations, 10–13. *See also* advisors; clients; communication strategies; complaints; financial planning; investigations; investment products; Know Your Client (KYC) form; risk profile; seniors; suitability; women clients

communication strategies: introduction and summary, 27, 42; action steps, 42–43; for asset concerns, 38; client assessments, 34–35; for lack of investment understanding, 40–41; for mistrust of advisors, 39; for privacy concerns, 38; probing for information, 36–38; references, 35–36; for secretive client, 34–39; time for relationship building, 30–33; trial periods, 35

complaints: introduction and summary, 213, 223; action steps, 224; appropriate responses to, 220–22; case study (Dank), 17–18; case study (Mrs. Koo), 214, 217–18, 230, 233–34; common defenses by advisors, 19–25; complaint letter, 217–20; definition, 215n2; notification of errors and omissions insurer, 222–23; with Ombudsman for Banking Services and Investments (OBSI), 235–37;

potential impacts, 68–69; reception of complaint, 213–20; resolution and settlement, 238–39; by telephone, 214–17. *See also* investigations; litigation

Conduct and Practices Handbook (CPH), 149–50

confirmation, by email, 110

credibility, 78–79. *See also* trust

CRM (Client Relationship Model), 11n4, 62n12

D

damages, 23n10. *See also* penalties; reimbursement; settlement

Dank (communication gap case study), 5, 6–7, 14–15, 16, 17–19, 20–21, 23, 24–25, 86

dealers: moving between, 69; operating model, 101; oral examinations by, 234–35; power of attorney and, 193

deception, 85, 234. *See also* secrecy

delegation, 61–62

dementia, 189–92

documentation: agenda, 107–8; client comprehension and questions, 108, 175, 179; collection of during investigation, 229–30; on computers, 95n2; confirmation emails, 110; for financial plans, 151–56; importance of, 20–21, 22, 24–25, 94; for investment products, 95, 104; telephone conversations, 216; two-way written communication, 109–10. *See also* Know Your Client (KYC) form

Dunne, Tim, 170–71

E

education, investor, 110–11

email communication, 110, 210

emotions, 126–28

engagement, 32–33, 80–83, 107, 158

expectations, 10–13, 157

F

face value, clients, 13–15

fee models, 62–63

fiduciary duty, 106, 106n14, 177–79, 205–6

financial planning: introduction and summary, 137–38, 160; action steps, 160; certification, 138n3, 141n5; clarification of obligations, 147–48; communication issues, 146–47, 156; completeness issues, 152–53; consistency issues, 153–55; correctness issues, 151–52; customization issues, 155–56; definition, 137n1; documentation issues, 151–56; engagement by clients, 158; expectations management, 157; importance of, 139–41; language issues, 148–49; limitations, 150–51; litigation against planners, 141–42; litigation based on plan, 142, 145–46; litigation case study (Giesbrechts), 142–45, 146, 148, 149, 158; as living document, 158–59; review process with clients, 158; risk reduction, 157–59; standards, 149–50; templates, 150

Financial Planning Standards Council (FPSC) Rules of Conduct, 149

Flank (communication gap case study), 5, 7–9, 14

fraud: action steps, 209–10; by family members and advisors, 206–8; identification of, 206; by strangers, 208–9

Fruit, Dr. (secrecy case study), 29, 37–38, 56

G

gender, 164–65. *See also* women clients

Giesbrecht, Mr. and Mrs. (financial plan litigation case study), 142–45, 146, 148, 149, 158

Gooshow (services rendered case study), 61

H

How to Get the Most from Your Financial Advisor (Bessner), 2, 243

Hurson, Tim, 170–71

I

incapacity/capacity, 189–92

income, client, 122–24

information, probing for, 36–38

insurance, errors and omissions, 222–23, 222n6, 228, 229, 235, 238

internet, 104

investigations: introduction and summary, 225, 241; action steps, 241; business changes and, 52n2; case study (Dank), 18–19; documentation collection, 229–30; lawyer retention, 226–29, 232, 235–36; letters from regulator, 227, 227n3; notification of SRO/regulator, 226; oral examination by dealer or regulator, 234–35; paper trail importance, 20–21, 22, 24–25; potential consequences, 226–27; reputational damage, 240; written responses, 230–34. *See also* complaints; litigation

investments: client lack of understanding and responsibility for, 40–41, 80, 83–84; onus of responsibility, 22–23; time for understanding, 31–33. *See also* investment products

Investment Industry Regulatory Organization of Canada (IIROC), 31–32, 198, 239–40

investment knowledge, 125–26

investment products: introduction and summary, 93–94, 113; action steps, 114; agenda for explanations, 107–8; case study (Mikka), 94–95; client engagement and, 107; client questions, 108, 109; client sophistication and, 105; confirmation emails and, 110; explaining to clients, 103–4, 107–11; in-person meetings and, 106; investor education, 110–11; managed products, 105; portfolio managers and, 106; practice for explanations, 103–4; questions to ask about, 99–101; research, 97–99, 104; responsibility to understand and explain, 101–2; risk assessment, 96–97; time for explanations, 107; two-way written communication and, 109–10; unsolicited trades, 111–13

investor education, 110–11

J

joint accounts, 202, 203–5

K

Kingsbury, Kathleen Burns, 166

Know Your Client (KYC) form: age, 119–20; Dank case study, 17–18; as defense against complaints, 19–21; demographic and factual aspects, 117–25; income clarification, 122–24; investment knowledge, 125–26; marital status, 120–21; name and background, 117–18; net worth, 124–25; power of attorney and, 192; residence, 118–19; risk assessment, 126–28; role in risk profile analysis, 117; updates, 86–90, 133n9; vocation, 121

Koo, Mrs. (complaints case study), 214, 217–18, 230, 233–34

L

lawyers, retention of, 226–29, 232, 235–36
legal advice, approach to, 4
letter, complaint, 217–20
licenses and certifications, 57–58
likes and dislikes exercise, 47–52
listening, 70, 73–74, 77–80, 117, 170
litigation: based on financial plan, 142–45; considerations, 16n7, 237–38; against financial planners, 141–42; hidden costs for advisors, 145–46. *See also* complaints; investigations
location, advisor, 60–61
loss tolerance, 129
Luca, Rosie, and Stubby (seniors case study), 184–88, 188–89, 193–94, 195–96, 203–4, 207
lying, 85, 234. *See also* secrecy

M

managed products, 105
marital status, client, 120–21
Marketplace (TV show), 31
meetings, 106, 156
Mikka (investment products case study), 94–95
Mookey, Mr. (secrecy case study), 27–29
Mutual Fund Dealers Association of Canada (MFDA), 31–32, 53n3, 198, 239–40

N

name, client, 117–18
net worth, client, 124–25
Never Be Closing (Hurson and Dunne), 170–71
newsletters, 109

O

Offering Memoranda (OM), 97, 98
Ombudsman for Banking Services and Investments (OBSI), 198, 235–37, 236n12, 237n13
Ontario Securities Commission (OSC), 31–32
oral examinations, 234–35

P

paper trail, *see* documentation

payment models, 62–63
penalties, 239–40. *See also* damages
play money defense, 23
portfolio managers, 106, 205n13
power of attorney (POA): authority and limits of, 195; client's best interests and, 195–96; client signature, 196; contact with client and, 197; fraud and, 208; importance of, 192–93; investment suitability and, 202–3; need to ask about, 193–94; signing for someone and, 168n14; triggers, 194
privacy, 38, 153, 188–89
probate taxes, 203
probing, for information, 36–38
problem solving, 71
prospectus, 97, 98

Q

questions, asking and documentation, 108, 109, 175. *See also* engagement

R

references, 35–36
referrals, 57n7, 68, 75, 166–67
regulators: letters from during investigation, 227, 227n3; notification during investigation, 226; oral examinations by, 234–35; penalties enforcement, 239–40
reimbursement, 215, 221–22. *See also* settlement
reputation, damage to, 240
residence, client, 118–19
risk: investment products, 96–97; lack of awareness by advisors, 53–56; setting expectations, 13
risk capacity, 129
risk composure, 129–30
risk need, 130–33, 199–201
risk perception, 130
risk profile, advisors, 52–53, 56
risk profile, clients: introduction and summary, 115, 134–35; action steps, 135; changes over time, 133; emotional factors, 126–28; loss tolerance, 129; management process, 133–34; purpose of, 128; risk capacity, 129; risk composure, 129–30; risk need, 130–33; risk perception, 130; for seniors, 198; willingness/unwillingness for risk, 128. *See also* suitability

risk tolerance, *see* risk profile
Rosie, Stubby, and Luca (seniors case
    study), 184-88, 188-89, 193-94, 195-
    96, 203-4, 207

S

secrecy: case studies, 27-29; communi-
    cation gap from, 15-16; strategies for
    dealing with, 34-39
self-awareness, *see* advisors, knowing self
seminars, 173
seniors: introduction and summary, 183,
    210; action steps, 210-11; capacity/
    incapacity, 189-92; case study (Rosie,
    Stubby, and Luca), 184-88, 188-89,
    193-94, 195-96, 203-4, 207; fiduciary
    duty to, 205-6; fraud, 206-10; investor
    education, 111; joint accounts, 203-5;
    power of attorney (POA), 192-97; pri-
    vacy rights, 188-89; risk profile, 198. *See
    also* suitability, for seniors
services rendered, 61-62
servicing practices, 69-71
Sessi (engagement case study), 80-81
settlement, 238-39. *See also* damages;
    reimbursement
Shank (communication gap case study),
    5-6, 9-10
Shnig, Mr. and Mrs. (risk needs case study),
    131-32
signatures: power of attorney, 196; signing
    for others, 88n8, 163, 168n14
Smee (know yourself case study), 45-46,
    50-51, 54
sophistication, client: assessment of, 102-3;
    claims to be unsophisticated, 108; docu-
    mentation of, 96n4; investment product
    comprehension and, 105; self-assess-
    ment of, 174n24; women clients, 173-77
spouse, death of, 202
strengths and weaknesses exercise, 47-52
Stubby, Rosie, and Luca (seniors case
    study), 184-88, 188-89, 193-94, 195-
    96, 203-4, 207
suitability: introduction and summary, 115,
    134-35; age, 119-20; demographic and
    factual aspects, 117-25; factors for fail-
    ure, 116; income, 122-24; investment
    knowledge, 125-26; marital status, 120-
    21; name and background, 117-18; net
    worth, 124-25; residence, 118-19; risk

assessment, 126-28; vocation, 121. *See
    also* risk profile, clients
suitability, for seniors: introduction, 197-
    98; age, 120; beneficiaries and, 202-3;
    capital preservation, 198; death of a
    spouse, 202; joint accounts, 202; risk
    need, 199-201; time horizon, 199

T

target market, 58-59
tax implications, for joint accounts, 203-4
teams, 63-64
telephone conversations, 214-17
terminology, 71
time: financial plan horizons, 154; horizons
    for seniors, 199; for relationship build-
    ing and product understanding, 30-33,
    70-71, 107
travel, 60-61
trial periods, 35
trust, 15-16, 39, 78-79, 170, 177
turnover, client, 58-59
two-way communication, 109-10

U

U, Mr. (unsolicited trades case study),
    111-13
unsolicited trades, 22-23, 111-13

V

vocation, client, 121
vulnerability, client, 177, 205

W

willingness/unwillingness, for risk, 128
women clients: introduction and summary,
    161-62, 181; action steps, 181-82; case
    study (Mr. and Mrs. Bunny), 162-63, 167,
    168-69, 180; changes for inclusion of,
    167, 179-81; fiduciary duty to, 177-79;
    financial understanding assessment,
    173-75; generalization issues, 169-73,
    175; importance of, 162; interest in
    learning by, 175-77; as invisible clients,
    168-69; neglect by advisors, 162-63;
    questions for, 175; referrals made by,
    166-67; risks with, 168-81; sophis-
    tication assessment, 173-77; wealth
    controlled by, 164, 165
written responses, 230-34

I would love to hear from you with a helpful review on Amazon letting me know what you thought of the book.

For volume discounts (more than 10 copies) of *Communication Risk* or to download the *Investor's Guide,* please visit:

www.BabinBessnerSpry.com

🐦 @BBSLitigation

f @babinbessnerspry

About the Author

E LLEN BESSNER IS an experienced, tough-minded, and common-sense commercial litigator with more than 25 years of practice at prominent Canadian firms, and now with Babin Bessner Spry LLP. Ellen has acted as counsel before Ontario courts of all levels, as well as at many arbitrations and regulatory proceedings, including before the IIROC, MFDA, OSC, and FSCO. Ellen is a leader in commercial and securities litigation, employment litigation, professional negligence, class actions, regulatory matters, insurance defense, and directors' and officers' liability, and she has regularly been retained to advise boards of directors and senior officers on issues of compliance.

At Babin Bessner Spry LLP, Ellen provides her popular and effective work in developing and presenting training and education programs for officers and directors, supervisors, and regulated professionals (financial and investment advisors, portfolio managers, insurance brokers and agents, supervisors and branch managers, and planners). The goal of these programs is to help reduce litigation and regulatory risk. Her programs include education and training on a range of liability, ethics, and compliance issues.

Ellen was appointed to the OSC's Seniors Expert Advisory Committee, was co-author of the paper "Current Practices for Risk Profiling in Canada and Review of Global Best Practices." You can learn more about her at www.babinbessnerspry.com.